Double Down

Double Down

*Reflections on
Gambling and Loss*

FREDERICK AND
STEVEN BARTHELME

HOUGHTON MIFFLIN COMPANY
BOSTON · NEW YORK
1999

For information about permission to reproduce
selections from this book, write to Permissions,
Houghton Mifflin Company, 215 Park Avenue South,
New York, New York 10003.

Library of Congress Cataloging-in-Publication Data
Barthelme, Frederick, date.
   Double down : reflections on gambling and loss /
Frederick and Steven Barthelme.
      p.   cm.
   ISBN 0-395-95429-0
   1. Compulsive gambling — Mississippi. 2. Compulsive
gamblers — Mississippi — Psychology. I. Barthelme,
Steven. II. Title.
RC569.5.G35B37   1999
616.85'841 — dc21   99-23957 CIP

Printed in the United States of America

Book design by Robert Overholtzer

QUM 10 9 8 7 6 5 4 3 2 1

CONTENTS

III

W E ARE BROTHERS, *college professors and writers,*
and for a period starting in 1995 we often played
blackjack all night long at the casinos in Gulfport and
Biloxi, Mississippi. At first we were playing on paychecks, our
tiny savings accounts, credit card advances, and we lost every-
thing we could get our hands on. Then, in 1995 and 1996, our
parents died, one after the other in quick succession, and after
that we gambled more, and harder. We lost everything they left
us, and then some. Still, we went on playing. We'd start at
eleven in the evening, play through the whole of the graveyard
shift, finish up at ten in the morning, or ten the next night,
always bleary-eyed and fatigued, pleased if we'd won, resigned
if we'd lost. This went on, became a routine, something we did
every couple of weeks, sometimes more often, sometimes less.
We'd go off it for a while, maybe months, then back to it, as
before. In the end, we were busted out of the Grand Casino at
ten in the morning on November 11, 1996, and later, indicted
and charged with felony conspiracy to defraud the casino. For
two years these widely publicized charges hung over our heads,
shadowing our every step, until, in the summer of 1999, the
Harrison County district attorney requested dismissal of the
case without a trial. On August 4, Judge Robert Walker, acting
on the D.A.'s request, dismissed all charges.

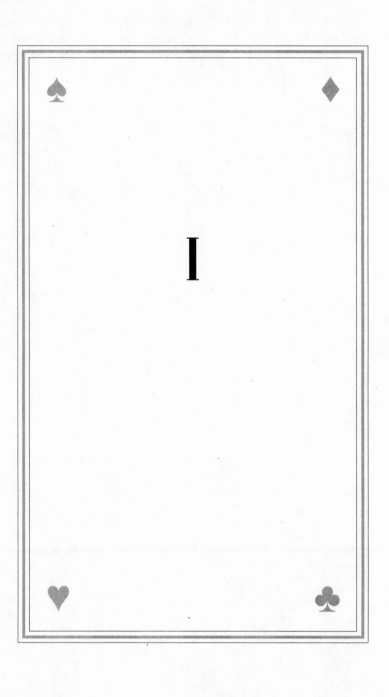

I

1

Mississippi

WE ARRIVED in Hattiesburg almost ten years apart. We'd held plenty of other jobs — cab driver, construction worker, advertising writer, journalist, art installer, architectural draftsman — and we'd each done stints at The Johns Hopkins University in Baltimore for graduate degrees, and now we were ready to settle down and teach.

Rick arrived first, in the mid-seventies, terrified because Mississippi had that reputation, that myth the prominent aspect of which wasn't the lovely Old South with its high manners and splendid architecture, but ignorance, burning, lynching. Being from Houston, having lived five years in New York City, and just out of graduate school, he figured he was profoundly enlightened and Mississippi wasn't. Indeed, his introduction to Hattiesburg was at an all-night gas station on Highway 49 where a lone teenager-slash-halfwit was capturing "pinching" bugs attracted by the bright lights and corralling them in a five-gallon bucket of sand he kept inside his little glass booth, a diversion he favored because, as he said, he liked to watch the bugs kill each other.

This was two in the morning, and Rick and his girlfriend

had been driving all day from Baltimore, where the morning before they'd had brunch with the British literary critic Tony Tanner in the polished-mahogany restaurant on the first floor of a hundred-year-old hotel. Now instead of talking about postmodernism they were facing it, and it didn't seem to know their names.

So Rick spent the first six weeks of his employment at the University of Southern Mississippi commuting from Houston, a safe four hundred and fifty miles away. In time he discovered that Mississippi was as civilized as anywhere else. The gas jockey notwithstanding, things had apparently changed, and at least in Hattiesburg and around the university, the myth was a phony. In fact, taken as a whole, the people he met in Mississippi began to seem gentler and more humane than many he'd run into in ostensibly finer settings. Probably there were remnants of the "old" Mississippi elsewhere in the New South of the seventies, but those remnants weren't on public view, did not seem dominant. In spite of the benighted reputation, Mississippi seemed more than its share enlightened.

Steve arrived nine years later, and if some of his impressions were different, maybe that was because when he arrived in Hattiesburg he had already spent the previous two years teaching at a university in Monroe, a dim, depressed, trash-strewn Louisiana town where even the snakes hung their heads. If the races seemed to him stiffer with each other in Mississippi than they had been in Louisiana, Hattiesburg itself was clean and bright, and the people were friendly. There was more money apparent, and the roads were mostly paved. During his first weeks in town he noticed two, maybe three Volkswagen beetles. You wouldn't have found them in Monroe.

So there we were, college professors and fiction writers. We were middle-aged, born in Texas, raised in a family of mostly fallen Catholics, with a father who was a successful and innovative architect and teacher, and a mother who was an English teacher and a reader, an actress in college who had wanted to pursue the stage but didn't quite escape the conventionality of her time. One older brother, Don, was a leading literary figure. Two other older siblings made their livings writing: Joan as a public relations vice president for Pennzoil Corporation, Pete as a Houston advertising executive and an author of mystery novels.

Growing up, we were trained in restlessness and doubt. Conformity wasn't prized. The house our father designed in 1939 — a large, low, flat-roofed box with a single small square room standing up on top — was an anomaly in a neighborhood of ranch-style and Tudoresque homes. Our house looked like a large, rectilinear *Merrimac*. On the empty grasslands west of Houston, it startled passersby.

The house had been made of wood alone, but later the exterior was covered in copper. Our father had this idea about copper. He had read that when sprayed with a certain acid compound, copper would discolor in a particularly attractive way, so he hired a contractor and several workmen and had the vertical siding covered in sheet copper. Then he bought a sprayer, a two-foot tank with a manual pump, and he mixed up a batch of the acid that was going to make the copper come alive in an exquisite turquoise. Well, it didn't happen. The copper asserted itself, and from that time forward the house was — exquisitely — brown.

Inside, it was a hotbed of modern furniture: elegant Saarinen chairs, the bent birch of Aalto dining tables and chairs, almost every piece of furniture or fabric that Charles and Ray Eames ever designed, from the little wire-frame footstools all the way up to, much later, the big rosewood and black leather chair, now ubiquitous. The rest of the furniture Father built himself, or had us build under his supervision. Things were always being redone, reconstructed, redesigned in accordance with some new idea he had.

We went to Catholic schools, and there, along with the conventional subjects, we were schooled in guilt. This was before traditional Catholicism lost its purchase, before "mea culpa" became "my bad," or however it's now translated.

The Catholics were good at their jobs. You're eight, maybe, and you go into your older sister's room and take a new yellow pencil away from her desk and erase some drawing you have been working on, and suddenly you think: *This is a sin. I'm stealing.* What you're stealing is eraser. But that's not the best part. The best part comes next, when the eight-year-old thinks: *No, this is prideful worry. Worrying too much about sins is a sin. It's "scrupulousness."*

For our purposes, the complaint that this indoctrination is barbarous is secondary to the idea that a Catholic education can accustom a soul to a high level of stimulation, and if you get too comfortable later in life, you miss it.

After high school, we each left our parents' house and the Catholic schools, Rick to Tulane, back to Houston, then New York; Steve to Boston, Austin, and California. We ran through three or four colleges apiece, worked different jobs, were rarely in the same city for more than a couple of months at a time, but over that period, in different ways we were doing the same thing: in fits and starts, we learned to write. Significantly, we learned the skill of editing — what our father was always doing with the house — which is in itself a school of dissatisfaction.

Years passed. We got older, more tired, less strident. We tried, not too successfully, to learn to lighten up. We went to Mississippi, where our lives were all aesthetics, literature, art, music, film, narrative, character, culture — teaching school. Books and movies in a pleasant town, handsome beyond what we had imagined, lush and green year-round, sixty thousand beings at the intersection of two highways. Originally a lumber and rail town, crossroads in a pine forest, Hattiesburg was a suburb attached to no city, distantly resembling some suburb of Houston twenty years before. Perfectly congenial, if a little short on excitement.

After teaching a few years, we had lost some connection with the world outside the academy, the ordinary world pictured in *USA Today*. We didn't drink very much, didn't smoke, took only sanctioned meds. Sex, drugs, and rock 'n' roll was a joke. We became, through no fault of our own, adults. Kids came to the writing program from all over the country, often from much better schools, and we helped them find things to write about, find their talents. We knew it was awfully sweet work, in our awfully sweet lives.

As college professors we were automatically in an out-of-harm's-way subculture, but we watched TV and read newspapers, so we had some idea of what the rest of the world was like. We just weren't *in* it exactly. In fact, maybe nobody of the middle class was much in it — that was the point of being middle class, yes? Buy your way out of the threatening and the immediate. The downside being that you lose some edge. In the worlds of kids or poor people or maniacs, there's always a lot of *stuff* happening, people doing crazy things, acting up, risking life, being desperately in love or terribly angry — a lot of stimulation.

So we nodded, and folded our hands, and *thought*. There inside our comfortable, well-maintained apartments. We lived in pleasant circumstances with work that was agreeable, but after all was said and done there was still this old furniture piled up in the garage — curiosity, recklessness, guilt. By training we were dissatisfied, by temperament restless.

Enter the boats. Sometime in 1992 casinos moved in on the coast and, observing a legal nicety requiring that casinos be waterborne — which was part of the bargain struck between the gaming lobby and the legislature to legalize gambling in Mississippi — they appeared as paddle wheelers that were docked against the beaches. They were cramped, crowded, intimidating. Long lines of customers waited just to get in, and inside the players were dead serious and going at full speed. The pit people were gruff and the atmosphere was sweaty and sleazy. If you sat down in front of a dealer, you'd better know what you were doing. But the boats *were* right there, and eventually we went to see what they were about.

The beaches had never been much good. The sand had been sucked out of Mississippi Sound and spread alongside Highway 90 like something in the bottom of an aquarium. It looked wrong, like a bad hairpiece. The water was the color of pot roast; locals said people loved Florida's emerald water, but fish, shrimp, and crabs preferred Mississippi's brown, where they were an industry. The towns strung along the coast had some of the dumpy charm of Galveston, where our father was born, where we'd visited our grandparents as children, and where we'd played on the winningly disheveled Stewart's Beach.

From Biloxi to Pass Christian to Bay St. Louis and Waveland, the coast towns were similarly distressed places, down at the heels, beat-up, and ugly, but now, with the advent of gaming (they love to call it *gaming*), the towns were tarting up in a new, too wholesome way. The cheesy glitz of minia-ture golf and bright pink seashell emporia gave way to paddle-boat quaint: cheap tux shirts, black bow ties, red cartoon suspenders. Gaming interests wanted casino gambling to seem harmless, fun for the whole family, so the newer developments worked along those lines. The architecture quickly turned Disneyesque: pirate ships and mock cowboy saloons slath-ered in happy neon (splashy pots of gold) instead of the tiny, furtive neon ("Nudes! Nudes! Nudes!") of the old beach-front strip. Mimicking Las Vegas, corporations were building twenty- and thirty-story hotels, huge parking lots, restaurants, and stores to attach to the casinos. They had day care if you needed it.

Biloxi had a great old restaurant called Fisherman's Wharf, a shoddy wood-frame thing built on telephone-pole pilings right on the sound. It had been serving seafood for more than forty years. Family-owned, dilapidated, but the food was marvel-ous in the way that only coastal dives can manage — fresh fish, fried chicken, big glasses of sweet tea. Gerald Ford had eaten there, and the restaurant had pictures of him arriving in a big limousine. Ford's plate was preserved behind glass, along with the silverware he'd used, his napkin, the menu he'd looked at.

After 1992, an Oriental-motif casino called Lady Luck ap-peared next door — a barge decked out like a Chinese res-taurant, complete with dragons and lanterns and fans. One Saturday when Rick and his girlfriend, Rie, were eating at Fisherman's Wharf, they spent the meal eyeing this new ca-sino. Afterward, they decided to give it a try.

Lady Luck was larger than the paddleboats — higher ceil-ings, more room. It was garish and silly inside, but it had charm. The Oriental decor was oddly coupled with loud pop music, waves of colored lights, and women in startlingly short skirts and tight tops. It was chilly in the casino, even in August.

Rick and Rie walked around, looked over the shoulders of the table-games players, tried their hands at video poker and the slot machines. They started with quarters and won a little, then moved up to half dollars and dollars. At a bank of dollar machines, one of them hit a small jackpot, and then the other hit one. Two sevens and a wild cherry. A minute later, Rick hit a five-hundred-dollar jackpot. Pretty soon they were carrying around buckets of dollar tokens, and gambling didn't seem so bad. They walked out with eleven hundred dollars of the casino's money, feeling as though they'd won the lottery. Eleven hundred dollars that wasn't theirs.

Later, a similar thing would happen to Steve and Melanie, his wife.

We learned that this was typical, that it happened just this way for a lot of people who went to casinos. You win something sizable, and thereafter gambling takes up residence in your imagination. You remember the visit. It's a key to the business — the first time you walk away with the casino's money. When we compared notes about these first trips, we indulged a light euphoria. Casinos were garish and grotesque and the people might be seedy, but the money was swell. We talked about buying books on slot machines, finding out which ones to play, what the odds were, how to maximize advantage and minimize risk. We were serious and excited; something new had come into our otherwise quiet lives. Neither of us had any idea how much those first jackpots would eventually cost.

2

Family

WHEN OUR eighty-seven-year-old mother entered a hospital in Houston on December 23, 1994, she was malnourished, unresponsive, only intermittently lucid. A week later she stopped eating, and shortly thereafter we allowed the doctors to install a feeding tube directly into her stomach. Before she was moved to a nursing home, she remained in the hospital for six weeks, attended daily by one or another of her children, sometimes her grandchildren, and only rarely by her husband. Our father could not abide hospitals and, further, was so much the rationalist or pragmatist that he would not "waste the time" sitting in a hospital room with a person who was increasingly absent, more often asleep than awake, and when awake not making all that much sense.

In his defense, when he was in the hospital, he didn't want anyone visiting him, either.

Weeks later, Rick was standing at the side of her hospital bed, speaking close to her face, watching her shut eyes, her lips only occasionally moistened by her tongue, and asked his mother what she was doing. He heard her reply, in a barely audible, eyes-tight whisper: "Suicide."

A nephew, sitting across the room reading a magazine, heard it differently, but Rick was certain: suicide was a powerful act of will that perfectly fit his mother. Her sickness, which had been accelerating for more than a year and which had been diagnosed as "white matter disease," produced in her many of the symptoms of Alzheimer's. She was tired of it.

That final trip to the hospital was rooted in a fall she took a couple days before we were scheduled to arrive in Houston for the Christmas holidays. The fall was followed, we were told, by a long and bitter argument with our father, this taking place mostly in the stairwell of their two-story townhouse apartment as he tried to get her upstairs to bed, and following that, a night and a full day of our mother's lying flat on her back and silent on the downstairs couch. Father finally got the sense to call our sister, Joan, and report that our mother had been "asleep" from four in the morning Sunday until six in the evening — fourteen hours — and that she seemed to be having trouble moving and talking.

After staying at her hospital bedside eight to ten hours a day from Christmas through the end of January, we gave up and returned to Mississippi.

In mid-February we made one more trip to see her in the nursing home. By that time she was a shriveled, curled-up, mummyish version of herself, and the rare sounds she made were no longer quite speech. At his office, the young gerontologist who by then was supervising Mother's care had the rest of the family convene for a meeting to determine whether the feeding tube that was keeping her alive should be removed.

If you've been in such a meeting, there's nothing to tell you about it; if you haven't, this seemed typical. The doctor sat at a

desk on which he had photographs of his family, and behind
him there were big windows with big plants beyond. Our
family was arrayed on a small couch and some extra chairs
hustled in for the occasion. Joan had secured this doctor. He
seemed fine to us, but there was something theatrical in this
meeting, some kind of horrible falseness. We had been through
a similar meeting with our brother Don's doctors in 1989. The
gerontologist wanted broad agreement before Mother was
taken off the tube and allowed to die. Father thought he
alone should be the one to decide. We asked, since the doctor
assured us she was not in pain, what harm would come of
waiting a few more weeks in the hope that she might improve. Something might change. We asked if that were impossible.

From the first, no doctor had identified any cause of her
failure, no heart attack or stroke, no reason that she should
just stop living. There was talk about whether a feeding tube
was or wasn't an "extraordinary measure," as defined in some
paper Mother had signed years earlier. The doctor, our father, and our two older siblings clearly felt that this should end
now, and the questions and speculations and what-ifs seemed
like non sequiturs. The meeting went on for twenty or thirty
minutes. Finally we had to say. He asked each of us directly,
one at a time, and it was three to two, which, the doctor said,
was not a strong enough endorsement to take any action.
Mother would live another few weeks. We drove back to Mississippi.

"Your mom," the doctor had said over and over in this meeting. "Your mom . . . this. Your mom . . . that." That was awkward. We never called her our "mom" that way, not without a
lot of spin on it, a joke or a sort of parody, probably because the

word, poisoned by advertising and political pieties, seemed too small for her. And if we did call her "Mom" sometimes, when we were kids or later, well, that was ours, that was private, like our affection.

We were inordinately attached to our mother, to both of our parents. We had girlfriends and wives but no children, no new families to replace the one in which we had grown up, so right on into middle age "the family" still meant them. For us, they hadn't been kicked upstairs to the no man's land of grandparenthood, and the family we'd grown up in was the only family there was. For us, even the nephews and nieces were outside the immediate circle — there were Mother, Father, and the five children, one of whom was already gone.

Mother died on March 13 — we'd gotten a telephone call from Joan. People in the English Department would stop us in the small entryway to the office and say, "I was sorry to hear about your mother." We'd say "Thank you" and recoil a little. It was too hard to receive their condolences which, while surely well intentioned, were nevertheless painful. Our colleagues would look at us and wait, and sometimes we didn't know how to behave or what they expected, because they did expect something in this normal transaction about a sad but ordinary event, an event they understood. When we could muster the appropriate rote responses — the thanks, the grave looks, the lowered head — everything went fine. But sometimes we couldn't get there, because to us this wasn't an ordinary event. To treat it this way, this public way, reduced it, and that was something our colleagues might have missed. We felt they did not understand how much we had loved our mother, how perfectly she had loved us. This seems presumptuous now, as if their mothers were not equally important to them, but then, in that moment, we weren't thinking about *their* mothers.

The loss of our mother and father in our own middle age — Rick was four years older than Steve — was a greater shock than might seem natural, because the family was an unnaturally large factor in our psychological arithmetic. Our colleagues didn't know that the family was the only society we'd always cared about since earliest childhood, held away from other people, safe harbor and seat of values, the one world we didn't want others presuming to speak of.

When Mother died we were fiercely quiet. People had spoken too much when our brother Don died. Two old friends — Roger Angell, Jack Barth — wrote brief, lovely eulogies. But Don was a minor public celebrity as well as a major figure in the literary community, and everybody wanted a piece of him. And took it, too, one after another. People who knew him casually or professionally published intimate poems and essays about him. People of the most tenuous acquaintance attached themselves ever so firmly in public after his death, distorting his memory, making a commodity of him for their own purposes. It was a messy thing and went on for years, until there was no more mileage to be wrung out of public mourning.

With Mother, the problem was not public; the problem was private. We were too close and too sensitive, and we didn't want anybody to mention her. Aside from Pete and Joan, the two of us, and Father, nobody deserved to.

While Father was clearly the provider and lawgiver of the family, Mother was its architect. The family was something she invented, shaped, guided, and protected as parent, pal, co-conspirator, nurturer, teacher, dresser, role model, route of all intercession, and unacknowledged giver of law to our father. She explained what needed to be explained, forgave what needed to be forgiven.

In her twenties, at the University of Pennsylvania, she was a handsome young woman from a working-class Philadelphia family who had somehow hooked up with our father when he transferred to Penn after having been asked to leave Rice University for some indiscretion in the school newspaper, which he edited — an indiscretion that wasn't his, as it turned out, but some fellow student's for whom Father was taking the fall. He was a fortunate man. When he went off to Penn, he found Mother and won her affection, a prize that took some winning, according to the family lore, for while Mother was smart, talented, stylish, attractive, and sought after, our father was only smart and talented.

Two or three years later, Mother left her adored mother and sister — our aunt Mike — and the rest of her known world to accompany her new husband to Texas, settling into a modest but newly remodeled and "modern" garage apartment behind his parents' house on Avenue I in Galveston. This was in the early 1930s. Don Jr. had been born in Philadelphia, and Joan was born in Galveston; the rest of us were born in Houston.

In a way, the family was two families, one with only two children and a second with the rest of us — Peter, Rick, and Steve. By the time we were old enough to pay attention, both Joan and Don were off at college; then, in the case of Don, in the army in Korea just after the armistice. After that, they were out in the world.

As children, we followed the adventures and successes of our older siblings as if they were scouts of the tribe, subjects treated biographically. Here they are, one after the other, editing their high school newspapers. Here's Joan in Europe, and here she is in Phi Beta Kappa. Here's Don editing the University of Houston *Forum*, and here, later, he's publishing his first tiny piece in *Harper's Magazine*. And now he's in New York. By this time, Pete was old enough to go off to Cornell and then to return to Houston to write advertising. We listened for his radio spots for Baby Giant Barbecue with the same regard with which we admired Don's short stories, by now appearing in *The New Yorker*. We thought all this was wonderful because our parents clearly thought it was wonderful. It's doubtful the young adventurers themselves celebrated their accomplishments with as much pleasure as did their mother and father, as one by one these accomplishments were reported back to the family for measure and appreciation.

Later, we would report in similar ways. In the family, it was what you did. It was as if the accomplishment itself were secondary. You went out and accomplished something so that you could report it, not to the world but to the parents, the family. In a story Mother liked to repeat, she was driving the carpool one afternoon when Steve was a high school freshman and he got in beside her, his friends in the backseat. Telling this story, Mother would mimic Steve in the front seat of the car, feigning his ridiculously rigid posture, eyes forward, a low voice contrived to make certain no one else in the car could overhear. "Guess who won the essay contest," she would mutter through unmoving lips. And then, shifting her blue eyes right and left a couple times, still imitating him, still acting: "I did." And then she would smile.

Though we felt a fierce tribal solidarity with Don and Joan, an engagement with their exploits and opinions, they were young adults and our experience was different. In our day-to-day life, our family was the three younger boys and Mother — Father having by then for the most part excused himself from the child-raising business to spend his energies on buildings he was designing and clients who needed endless care and persuasion.

Perhaps that was just as well. Later, when we were grown, our oldest siblings often alluded to the terror of our father's attention in *their* childhoods, a kind of vague, best-left-unsaid eyebrow-raising that effectively communicated the terrifying things they had once been subjected to at his hand. This treatment was not a minor matter. It was presented as the origin of and the reason for an anger that sometimes marked their attitudes toward Father, anger that by the evidence of our eyes seemed only to go one way: our father meant them no harm. It was nothing so fashionable as "abuse"; this was a kind of excessive parenting or psychological aggression, the talking curse, and to us it remained a mystery.

While we well knew Father could be harsh if we caught his attention in some unhappy way, we could never imagine the terror suffered by our older siblings, what it was that had been different enough from our own childhood experiences to explain their long-carried anger. When we asked, even well into adulthood, we were always rebuffed — no one could specify what our father's unspeakable practices were. The only firsthand evidence we had of their childhoods were quaint old photos of them in odd shorts, or in Sunday getup in the firm grip of a wonderfully mysterious-looking Mother, or with a silent-film-style Father. There was even a black-and-white eight-millimeter home movie, a Chaplinesque affair in which Father, in the best homemade tradition, is shown attempting to take a photograph of Don and Joan, and failing. It seems they couldn't stand still. So Father ends up chasing them, camera and tripod poised as if to strike, in burlesque circles around some horse statue on the Rice University campus.

Remembering this movie and the snapshots, and thinking back on our own childhoods, we still wondered what our oldest brother and only sister could have been talking about. Our childhoods were crowded with chores and dinner-table stories of rotten contractors, but nothing that approached horror.

Which is not to say our father was a walk in the park in our childhood, only that if he was a terror, he was so in a way not too difficult to understand even at the time. We shoveled more oyster shell for the driveway, hauled more sand in wheelbarrows, carried more bricks for his endless rebuilding projects, did more chores by a factor of five than any of our childhood friends and neighbors, and we came in for much more than our share of ridicule. Our father was very good at ridicule, and he used it far more than was healthy or necessary, often inflicting pain that was later assuaged by our mother's kindness and patience.

The heart of it was a sort of profound disappointment that Father could effortlessly project, as if by sheer inadequacy you had let him down in some terrible way when all you had done was fetch the wrong pair of pliers from the tools on the back porch. "Not *those* pliers," he would say, coupled with a hasty glance (suggesting how important whatever he was in the middle of was), and the look and the tone of voice made you feel as if you were the stupidest bag of dirt in a world of bags of dirt. It was perhaps worse that, toward bigger events — you wreck the car, you flunk out of college — he was remarkably tolerant.

Father was the first adventurer in the family, the hero of his self-created myth; it was his name we first found wonderful when we read it in the papers, his accomplishments the first carefully shown us. Part of this myth was the great man brought down by *them*, the venal and stupid people with whom he had to deal. Like most myths, this one was not altogether untrue. But it did put a fine, perhaps even a desperate, edge on his children's wish to measure up. To be stupid, to disappoint him, would make us just like *them*.

So ours was a slightly irregular family, made peculiar by these two extraordinary people. Father and Mother were remarkable in different ways: our father was an innovator, a pragmatist who would shoot a new hole in a four-foot-square plate-glass window with a BB gun to prove that the existing hole in the glass, the one he was duplicating, had been made from the inside, not the outside, and was thus the work of one of us guilty children; he thought highly of thinking and was very good at it. Our mother was like an act of spiritual perfection, the kindest, wisest, most forgiving, most beautifully balanced person we ever knew.

Once, home from college when he was about nineteen and she was fifty-nine, Steve tried to talk her into trying marijuana. Standing in her kitchen, Mother laughed, asked some questions, turning it over in mind for more than a few minutes, and finally shook her head. "It just wasn't something you did," she said, "when I was growing up."

Trained as a teacher and an actress, she was an elegant, strikingly handsome woman well into middle age, possessed of "a wicked wit," as Don said of her in an interview, and ready always to care about what her children cared about, from books to boa constrictors. She liked to play. Somewhere in the box of home movies is one Rick and Steve made as children, a private-eye parody in which Mother, about age fifty, does a turn as a drunken barmaid wearing a beret and smoking a pipe. She was up for just about anything. The only thing you could not do around Mother was criticize one of her children.

In the seventies, eighties, and nineties, Christmas was the only time of year when the family made an effort to get together. We returned to Houston, planned the holiday around the ritual Christmas Eve celebration at which twenty-odd people — the seven of us, and husbands and wives, grandchildren, nieces and nephews — gathered in the living room of our parents' townhouse apartment for the giving of gifts, and the next day for Christmas dinner. This was the last public symbol of the powerfully influential sense of family that had always governed our lives.

Don's death from cancer in 1989 was the first blow to the family's solidarity. While he and our father were not particularly close, he was close to the rest of us, and to everyone his death was a startling reminder of where we were and what we had to look forward to. His absence threw the family out of balance, as if one of the actors in our drama had walked off-stage in the middle of the third act, leaving the rest of us to stare at one another, wondering how to continue.

If Don's death was not a sufficient blow to destroy the family, it did suggest what being hit hard might feel like. In the nineties, our mother and father became more frail, forgetful, argumentative, wispy. Christmas rituals continued but were increasingly strained and difficult. The gifts were perfunctory, the habitual gatherings stilted, the jokes weary. The sense of this group of people as a *family* slipped away. When our mother entered the hospital at Christmas in 1994, we all knew that the family that had so long nurtured and supported us, from which we had always taken, and still took to a surprising degree, our self-definition, our sense of self, was going down hard, fast, final.

In the hospital in the long days of January, Rick had talked to Mother, when she would talk, about how she felt, whether she wanted anything, trifles, just to talk. In the early evening of January 6 she woke up a little hazy. "Remember who I am?" Rick asked.

"Yes, dear," Mother replied.

"So, who?"

"You're Ricker."

"Do you know where you are?"

"Yeah."

"Where?"

"My mother's house."

"Where is your mother's house?"

"In Philadelphia."

"How old are you?"

"I don't know."

"Do you remember what year this is?"

"Yes."

"What?"

"Nineteen . . ."

"Mother? Where are you?"

"Phil-a-ma-dinx."

"Nope. You're in St. Luke's Hospital in Houston."

She was silent.

"Do you want some soup? Anything?"

"No. Not really."

"How do you feel?" Rick asked.

"With my fingers," she said, gripping his hand.

Two months later she died. And when she shut her eyes, she closed them not only on the mechanics and machinery of the nursing home, not only on the ordinary world, but also on the world she had made for the rest of us — our father, our siblings, ourselves. She disappeared and took with her the creation that had defined and enriched our lives up until that time: her family. We were on our own in a remarkable new way, and we were not ready.

3

Tearing Down the House

IN THE FIRST few years after the boats came to the coast, we gambled when we could. We played at Gulfport, Biloxi, Natchez, and Waveland, but we didn't play for much — a couple of hundred dollars here and there.

It was entertainment. We'd go in, wander around, play the slot machines, play video poker, tell jokes, go home. Once, when Rick lost six hundred dollars in Natchez, it seemed as if the sky had fallen. He and Rie walked back to the wonderful old Eola Hotel, where they had a top-floor room with a view of the Mississippi, and Rick promised that his gambling days were over. This was a promise he would make often.

Then, in 1995, after our mother died, the gambling got meaner. No longer content to play the little slots, we played the five-, ten-, and twenty-five-dollar machines. It wasn't enough to play the five-dollar blackjack table; we moved up to the "salon," where the minimum bet was twenty-five dollars and the tables were dressed in glamorous purple felt. Each seated five players, not the seven of the nickel tables. We started playing bigger money, harder money, and making friends at the casino. The hosts would greet us when we walked in; the dealers would stop what they were doing to say hello as we passed their tables; the cashiers knew us by name and were eager to slide our credit cards through their machines. Everyone seemed to like us, so we became regulars at the Grand in Biloxi, and later at the Grand in Gulfport.

We won sometimes, even four or five trips in a row, taking home hundreds of dollars of the casino's money, but always there would come that trip when the losses were catastrophic — two or three thousand dollars, losses that easily eliminated the winnings of the previous nights.

There was a new intensity to our play, something so subtle that we only vaguely noted it, putting it down to a combination of factors — a feeling that we ought to be able to figure out a way to win, coupled with the knowledge (from the books we'd been reading) that we probably weren't going to win and, added to that, the recognition that our gambling wasn't sensible, though sensible counted less now that Mother was dead.

We might not notice the intensity of what we were doing until we were on the way home, down fifteen hundred dollars. Or it might appear in the way we cursed the slot machine that we'd just hit for a big jackpot, while we were waiting for the little ceremony of the cash payoff and the W-2G tax form. It might be felt when we pushed whatever money we had left — three hundred-dollar bills, say, or a couple of twenties — out onto a spot at a blackjack table and said, "Money plays," a loser's custom we made our own.

At the table, losing our money, we were all smiles, as if it were nothing. In fact, it felt like nothing. Money isn't money in a casino. At home, you might drive across town to save a buck on a box of Tide, but at the table you tip a cocktail waitress five dollars for bringing a free Coke. You do both these things on the same day.

We were trained in feigned indifference. Everyone did it, but for us it was a family thing, helped you get by in the family. Lots of fast folks in the family, people who were always thinking, always ahead of you, so what we practiced was making everything look like nothing, smoothing stuff out, taking things in stride. Do otherwise and you were vulnerable, at risk, somebody was sure to make a joke at your expense. So you level everything out; you don't get too excited, don't get too let down. Once you master the drill, everything is equal and you don't get cut up too bad. You won't lose an argument because you can *not care* your way out. Day to day, no matter what went before our eyes, this queer *moderation* became a well-worn defensive weapon.

But that wasn't the end of it. Rationality was prized, but so was intensity. Feeling was admired and given broad authority, but any *display* of feeling tended to get mocked. One afternoon, in late adolescence, Rick stormed out of the house, shouting and kicking out a plywood panel in the back porch screen door. Father said, "Rick? Do you want me to call you a doctor?"

Thereafter, the phrase "Do you want me to call you a doctor?" became code in the family. All employed it, often gleefully.

We cared a great deal about things, because that was what you were supposed to do, but the caring made us vulnerable, both inside the family, which was pretty much a nonstop you-blinked game played by seven people, and in the outside world as well. Appearing to be blasé — indifferent, relaxed, casual, unconcerned — was essential protective coloration disguising this vulnerability. And we noticed, too, that out in the world there was something suspect about the feelings conjured by people who were always declaring and displaying the bigness of their emotions. The feeling of an emotion almost seemed to preclude the expression of it, so when we ran into declaration and display, we discounted the quality of the underlying feeling.

Self-consciousness played a part. In the family you were surrounded by people who seemed able to read your mind, and what might have been worse, cared enough to *want* to, with the predictable result of an intense self-scrutiny, which was in turn amplified by training in Catholic schools that suggested God Himself spent much of His time on your shoulder, evaluating and judging your every move.

For these and other trials, appearing blasé took the place of more standard protections, like powerful religious faith or ideological righteousness, class snobbery or contentious sophistication, those happy spiritual add-ons that serve to free us from thinking too much about what we're doing. Although we had some of those protections, we didn't believe any of them sufficiently to forget how psychologically visible we were, how mixed our motives often were, or how often we would lose the other you-blinked game, the one being played outside the family, where people really didn't care.

As card-carrying Barthelmes we believed two things, although neither provided adequate emotional cover: first, that we could "understand" things and thus tame them, and second, that words, adroitly deployed, were a bullfighter's cape — they allowed you to step aside and avoid the horns of a threatening experience. It helped to have something smart to say, though that wasn't essential, since it wasn't the quality of the thought that was key, just that the thought was always there, between you and *it*.

This was the system: understanding in the sense of *accepting*, the first step of which was *putting words to* whatever happened as quickly as we encountered it, instantly. We lived these self-conscious lives, always prepared for the worst, always "pleased" by the best.

When our mother died, we understood. We had plenty of time to go through the stages you're supposed to go through when someone close to you dies, so after a while it became reasonable in its way. Her death eventually made a certain kind of sense — when her body was so frail we couldn't even imagine her recovering. Shortly after that she was dead, and the first, most obvious part was over.

Father's death was brutal in a different way. An Indian woman who worked for him in Houston called Rick long distance and said, "I'm afraid there has been some trouble with your father."

Rick, thinking his father might have taken a fall, said, "Oh, yes? Trouble? What?"

She said, "He died this morning."

This call came around noon on July 16, 1996. The peculiarity of the exchange with the woman was not lost on Rick; the concept "some trouble with your father" had taken on new meaning. Now it was burlesque. And instantly, before the phone was back in its cradle. Just as quickly, he realized he was paying attention not to his father's death but to the odd report of the kind, efficient, *foreign* health-care worker.

He got on the phone and called Steve.

After that, we got in touch with Pete and Joan. We were already planning the trip. No one from the family still lived in Houston; no one else would take care of our father's things. Rick was Father's executor, and the two of us from Hattiesburg would have to leave for Houston, eight hours away, that afternoon. Like in a spy movie, we were "cleaners" — our job was to go in, take care of the mess, and get out. Father was the last of the original Barthelmes in Houston, and when we were done, there wouldn't be a trace of us left, which mattered to no one but us, and to us only in its echo of a past time when the city was an integral part of the family, part of our sense of something that might last forever.

The drive over was eerie — a little too familiar, too commonplace. We stopped for hamburgers at the Burger King in Crowley, Louisiana, just as we'd always done when driving to Houston for Christmas and summer visits. We spent time acquainting ourselves with our father's death, trying it on, getting the sense of it. When we got to his apartment, the bed things were all clean and folded on the bare mattress in the living room. Just like in the movies. A dead man's bunk. He had moved downstairs, been living down there, not using the second floor where the bedrooms were. His — our, the — dining room table was covered with papers, a big checkbook, reminder lists, worn twenty-year-old green file folders labeled "Bills," "Investments," "Gas & Electric," neatly arranged. Everything orderly. His wallet, his keys. His financial records. That first night, sitting with nothing to do in the silent apartment, we glanced through the files, looking for wills and codicils, debts, deeds. When everything was done, it seemed the remaining four children would inherit more than half a million dollars.

We went by the funeral home where he had been taken. Inside, it was heavily decorated, but it didn't have much in the way of furniture. There were too many walls and no people, the place seeming oddly off duty as we sat in the exaggerated air conditioning of one of the little offices, waiting for someone to arrange for cremation and burial. We didn't ask to see our father, and no one asked if we wanted to. Back at the apartment, Steve wrote an obituary — "beloved artist, teacher and father."

We spent a week cleaning up the place, tearing down things Father had built there: drafting tables, an elaborate stereo system, special cabinetry. We emptied the closets, tossing everything we could bear to toss. We threw away beds, pots and pans, half-filled bottles of liquor, paper, pens, and pencils. We threw away soap, salt, houseplants, toothpaste, towels, Windex, zinc ointment.

There were some psychological slips. On the fourth day, Steve was in the upstairs office working on the trash lumber for more than an hour, using a couple of Father's screwdrivers and a claw hammer to remove the nails and screws from the stacked pine and plywood of the already disassembled homemade filing cabinets and tables, working maybe a half hour ahead of the guy coming to haul it all away to the dump. There was no good reason to remove a single nail; that fact didn't stop him.

We piled clothes and junk we didn't want on our parents' bed, waiting for the Salvation Army. Some things of our mother's we packed up in boxes: slippers, dresses she wore often, some jewelry, a coffee cup. We did the same for Father, though we picked different things. Not his clothes or shoes or leather jacket, though we did save his hat, the comical gray leather cap he once wore on his walks, cocked back on his head. The other things we picked for him were architectural design books — Corbu and Mies, Gropius, Neutra, Wright, Aalto — and objects that were special to him or seemed especially like him. His Leicas. A seventy-year-old handsaw that had belonged to his father, who had owned a lumberyard in Galveston.

We spent long days packing, dismantling, discarding. With

each thing discarded, we pushed past a slight resistance, an instant or less than that, and the thought of how this or that had mattered to our parents. We were throwing away their whole lives. But there was too much of everything. We had already packed dozens of boxes of things we knew no one would ever use or even look at, things like the seventy or eighty reel-to-reel recordings of operas, in their white boxes, numbered in Father's precise architectural hand.

It was hard work, sweaty work, and it ran from ten o'clock in the morning until two or three the next morning, seven days solid. Our father and mother had lived in the apartment twenty years. They were dug in. We didn't weep; grief took the form of work, of maniacs crating and carrying and dragging stuff to the dumpster, wrapping and packing and labeling. Nonstop. One of our nephews came over one day, and another day Pete drove in from his new place down the Texas coast, but mostly it was just the two of us in that apartment where we'd visited our parents over the last twenty years, erasing them bit by bit.

We shared the job of executor. We did it as our father might have done it, probably not as thoroughly but with every bit as much organization. We had spreadsheets in Excel. We wrote letters in triplicate and quadruplicate. We saved copies of notarized papers. We called some godforsaken cemetery somewhere south of Galveston where Father's parents were buried, because one of the notes in Father's files listed two cemetery plots there as an asset. We corresponded with the people at the cemetery, and they reported that the plots weren't worth all that much. We found out the value of Father's Leicas, how much we might sell them for, which we never had any intention of doing. We divvied up the cash, set up separate accounts for the bonds, offered Pete and Joan whatever they wanted of the furniture and the rest. They took a few photographs, nothing else.

In a way, that was reasonable. All the fancy furniture — Aalto, Saarinen, Eames, Mies — was old and had seen much wear. Still, for the two of us doing the cleanup work, we didn't so much want to look away from the family as to stare at it, feel it in all the *stuff* in that apartment, touch it, remember it, steep in it. Rationally, of course, carefully and passively noting each find — the family Bible neither of us knew we had, pictures of our mother's family, a copy of our mother's grandfather's will on crinkly blue paper, keys to unknown locks, old suitcases we once played with, books, tools, files, letters to and from family members, Mother's red flannel robe, the one she always wore around Christmas. These were things our parents had cared about, touched; forgetting was the last thing on our minds.

The family was too rich, too much in our blood, too much with us all the time. We had no place to go. We were too much *of the family*. We owed too much to Mother and Father. We cared too much, were too deeply invested in them to have them die. All the practice we had at making things equal, at making everything the same, at normalizing experience, came into play that week. We buried them in boxes of photographs and slides and cameras, boxes of letters, boxes of books, boxes of stereo equipment, boxes of architectural drawings, boxes of special clothes and knickknacks and old magazines with Father's "fame" in them.

Figuratively, we buried our parents in brand-new cardboard boxes, stacked the boxes neatly in the apartment, numbered each one of them, detailed their contents on the outside. We planned, made lists, telephoned, decided, bought, shipped, shrugged, worked together. Unconsciously, unaware, this was a weeklong funeral, a ceremony modeled not on ordinary funerals but on the projects of our childhood, the times the family would pull together for some house or landscaping work, or an architectural competition Father might have been doing, or even preparations for hurricanes the radio was sure were coming straight up Galveston Bay. For these projects, everyone would be assigned tasks, day after day, and the air was electric with the importance of the undertaking, and we were a goddam army.

So we were when tearing down the house. And finally, after visits from Goodwill, the Blue Bird Circle, some guy who'd done hauling for Pete years before, and a final walk-through by the movers, we were back on Highway 10, headed home, our parents relegated to the boxes. A week later, Bekins movers made it to Hattiesburg, to Outback Storage, unit 233, a place for our parents in perpetuity, a modern-day mausoleum where we could visit. As if they were Egyptian royalty, we buried their property, their jewels, their tools, and their stationery, and for months afterward we went to the shed, mostly late at night — two, three, four in the morning — unlocked the padlock, lifted the rolling steel door, clicked on the light with the fifteen-minute timer, and walked among the boxes of papers and photographs and clothes, among the chairs we'd saved, the dining table padded with packing quilts, the Laverne-covered folding screen Father had built, the marble slab that had been a coffee table.

Now they were dead and buried, and we were alone and middle-aged, and nothing really mattered all that much anyway. They had seen us through to comfortable adulthood. We had seen them through to death.

Our family had started dying a few years earlier, and pointlessness forced itself on our attention. We were probably more vulnerable than most because we were not well prepared. Unlike many people we had known — friends, wives, casual acquaintances — our family had had awfully good luck, been blessed with good health, long life.

Don was not supposed to die; he was only fifty-eight. There were terrible weeks of waiting and hoping, of doctors and ideas, of trying to *think* him back to health, and of watching the grueling effects of his dying on our mother. We had not been taught and never learned well how to not pay attention. Paying careful attention and "facing facts" was what we had been trained at, and now what we had to attend to was dying, which itself lacks logic and gives a senseless or ridiculous tinge to everything else. First Don, then Mother, then Father. Even though we still talked to our parents in our heads, and often, we knew where they were. They were ashes in two encyclopedia-size boxes sunk in a low artificial ridge just off the Dallas Freeway. That's where they are now.

If after our mother died the gambling grew meaner, with more frequent trips to the boats and bigger stakes, sixteen months after that, when our father died, the intensity rose again. Not only was our interest fiercer, but now we had an inheritance, a considerable sum of money, a new war chest.

On the drive down to the casinos in the middle of the night, we talked all the time about why we were going, why we liked it, why we went when we knew we would lose, how we imagined it possible that we could win. When our parents came up in the conversation on those drives — an hour and a half with the tires sizzling on the concrete and the fog so thick that taillights emerged suddenly in front of us like UFOs — the talk grew short, tight, and clean; not much needed to be said. Between us was an extraordinary understanding, a shared knowledge, a common experience, harmonies of sadness, melancholy, loss. So the discussion was sketchy. Just what was needed. To be in that car driving to Biloxi or Gulfport knowing we both held in special, separate but similar affection, love, and esteem both of our parents — our beloved mother, whom no one could not love, and our beloved father, whom no one could quite love enough — knowing how crippling their deaths were for each other was hugely reassuring.

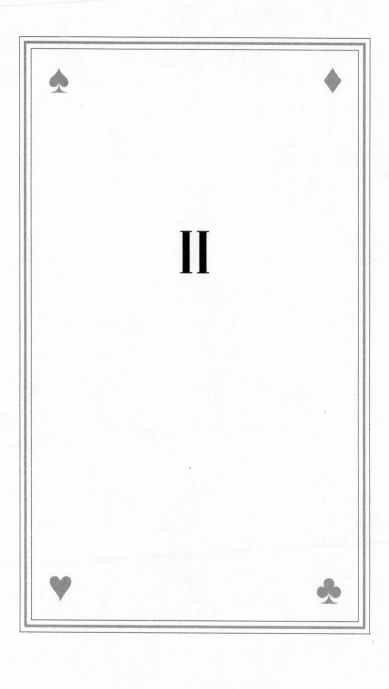

II

4

One Night

RICK TELEPHONES Steve just after midnight on a Wednesday. Rick has finished his classes for the week. Steve has done one class Thursday, but it's a night class. Rick says, "So, let's roll. I want to be back by six."

"A.M.?" Steve says. "Never make it."

"Sure we can," Rick says. The conversation wanders a few minutes, neither of us ready to decide. Rick says, "Let me call you back. Let me think and call you back."

It's routine. Rick calls, makes the suggestion. Steve hangs up the phone, asks Melanie if she wants to go. She doesn't.

"When are you going?" she says.

"He's calling back," Steve says. He goes and changes into a heavy shirt with flaps over the pockets — it's cold in the casinos and the pocket flaps hide the hundred-dollar bills he always ends up carrying. He returns to the kitchen and puts his credit cards in a stack on the table.

"Call me when you get down there," Melanie says.

Across town, Rick imagines how Rie will react to another midnight trip to the coast. If he wins, he's discovered, she hates it less.

Rie lives in another house, with her daughter and their two dogs. She doesn't like the gambling; she doesn't want Rick gambling ever. But after months of arguing she has given up. "It's your money," she says. "Throw it away if you want to." He can't call Rie now, because she's asleep.

He picks up the phone and calls his friend Mary Robison, a gambling buddy and a colleague at the university.

"We're thinking of going to the coast," he says.

"We shouldn't," Mary says.

"Yeah, I know," he says. "But we are. I'm calling Steve back. We're leaving right away. You want to go?"

"I'll take my car."

"If Steve wants to stay longer, he can have mine and I'll come back with you. That okay?"

"Fine with me," she says. "I like to drive."

In the car, headed out Highway 49, we stop at an Exxon station for gas and Cokes and then head into the darkness in a short parade. Rick's car, Mary's car.

The night is clear, and once we're out of town we see stars overhead, in between the rows of pine trees. The north-south lanes of the highway are separated by a fifty-foot green space planted with hundred-year-old pines. Some have been cleared close to Hattiesburg, but farther down the highway toward the coast the trees are still there. On either side of the road, more pines. At first the conversation in Rick's car is sparse. A few remarks about this or that graduate student, this or that short story, a thesis defense coming up, and eventually the talk comes around to a particularly fine story by one of the graduate students. Both of us are surprised by this work, surprised that this student is capable of writing so well. It gives us a sense that what we do might be worth doing.

Moments later we are making fun of some of our colleagues,

repeating characteristic remarks in mock imitation like catty high school girls. There's more to it than that — there's disappointment. Many of these colleagues used to be better, before years of talking to students who were too easily impressed. It's an occupational hazard of teaching.

For a while this ungenerous exercise is entertaining. Then we ride quietly, the tires humming on the concrete. It's all darkness, high pines, until Steve says, "What'd you lose last week?"

"Twenty-four," Rick says.

"After everything?"

"Yeah, twenty-four. I was up a thousand, lost it on a couple hands," Rick says. "If I could just keep from chucking all the money out on the table."

"That'd be good," Steve says. "Still, sometimes you win."

"Oh, yeah," Rick says.

"If I can hit a slot for a couple grand right away, I'm usually good for the night," Steve says.

"How often has that happened?"

"Frequently. That's a regular event."

Rick is watching his rearview, keeping an eye on Mary, to be sure she's following, identifying her car by the shape and placement of its parking lights. "How frequently?" he says.

"About twice," Steve says. "Two times," he adds, for clarification.

There are a lot of trucks on the highway. They are all new, white and clean and tall, and they roar when they go by. Rick says, "I'm going to keep it to twenty-five tonight. If I lose twenty-five, I'm getting Mary to take me out."

We drive on in silence. Alone and yet together, and the night seems very big. It goes on for miles. The land is low rolling country and all we see are the trees alongside the highway, the occasional truck, the occasional roadside stand. We pass Wiggins, a town thirty miles south of Hattiesburg. We pass Perkinston, a junior college. We pass the pine-milling operation, acres of it right by the highway, where the huge, forty-foot-long trunks of pine trees are turned into two-by-fours. Across the road there's a motel where, on Sunday afternoons, we used to take a room to see Oilers football games on TV.

We pass the Bible store — "Thousands of Bibles in Stock!" — and cruise through the little all-night town by the bend in the highway — one building, a small white store with two restaurants, and a state trooper's car. Steve's got his eyes shut, forcing himself to rest. Rick punches the cruise control at seventy-two, seven miles over the limit.

When we reach the highway sign that says twelve miles to I-10 and fourteen to Gulfport, Steve calls his wife. "We're at the twelve-fourteen sign. We'll be there shortly." This is more of the routine.

We drive through the outskirts of Gulfport and under Interstate 10, then straight down to the Gulf. Highway 49 dead-ends at the water, at a dilapidated turquoise beachfront marina and amusement park, the one Donald Trump was supposed to buy for his casino. We turn and drive and eventually hit ours. In the garage, we find a first-floor parking space, tuck the car in for the night. Mary's tires squeal as she backs up and finds a parking spot of her own.

The walk from the garage to the casino is all nerves, like a football player's walk from the locker room to the field. We swagger, we lope. It's jokes and jitters. We imagine tall stacks of chips. Good cards could come. Everything is still possible.

"Start slow," Steve says, cautioning Rick against his tendency to jump the bet early.

"Yeah, yeah, I know," Rick says.

Mary says, "I can't afford to lose a penny. I've got forty dollars here and I can't afford to lose a penny." She's tough, tall, good looking but deadly thin. In her black clothes she looks like scaffolding.

"You've only got forty dollars?" Rick says.

"That's all I've got in my pocket," she says, pretending this is a very important distinction. "I've got my credit cards. But I can't lose a penny," she says.

Mary often says things because she loves the way they sound. She loves the word "penny."

The casino floats atop sloppy water you wouldn't want to fall into. Huge concrete piers anchor the "boat." Because casinos can't be on Mississippi land, the owners dig out huge pits on the beachfront, flood them, float these barge-casinos there. Then they dress them up in neon and flashing lights and hot designer colors, only a few feet from Mississippi soil. We cross the carpet-covered metal gangplank, nod at the white-shirted security guard there with his chrome clicker. Three quick clicks and we're counted. Then it's only the doors between us and the air conditioning and the noise and the screeching players and the ingratiating dealers and the thick swirled carpet and the floating scent of a thousand people smoking. It's at this point things change.

Steve swears it's the air conditioning. As soon as it hits you, he says, you're gone. We open the doors and we're washed with treated air, the din, the scent of money, liquor, smoke. Adrenaline and after-shave. We're keyed up now, hopeful. We walk with a sure step and purpose. Something is suddenly clear, precise, desired.

Almost as soon as we're inside the casino, we split up. Rick heads off to the cashier's cage, Mary peels to one side, to a row of dollar slot machines, Steve heads for an ATM far down on the other side, ignoring the one by the doors. With a wave, we lose sight of one another, vanish into the crowd. It's a Wednesday night, it's two in the morning, and there are plenty of people gambling. People who, after a time, blur together, along with the wins and the losses, as they do in this entire tale, in which days and nights have been compressed, talk has been approximated, names have been changed.

Steve gets four hundred on a credit card to go with the six in cash he has brought with him. He remembers when he first started gambling, how he laughed when he saw ATM machines in the casino, how he had made himself a rule never to use an ATM there. He was very serious then. He remembers thinking, That's death. He walks over to a one-dollar video poker machine and sits down. Playing dollars is a sort of therapy, to get his bearings. After ten or fifteen minutes he'll try some five- and ten-dollar slots, in the hope of hitting an early score to set up the night. Then, win or lose, he'll move on to blackjack.

The first poker machine eats his twenty-dollar bills, six or seven hands with never better than a pair, which only gives you your bet back. A flush would pay four times the bet, a full house nine, returning forty-five dollars on a five-dollar credit bet. Steve tries the machine next to the one he started on and it's no better. Pair of jacks, nothing, nothing, nothing, nothing, more jacks, nothing, nothing. He closes his eyes, trying not to think that this is one of those depressing nights when all he does is lose and lose some more. You can stand losing the money if at some moment or for some period of time there is actual hope, a winning streak, jackpots, piles of chips, laughter.

He gets up and walks over to a bank of five-dollar slot machines near a roulette table, looks up and down the row for a machine that's paid off the last few times he's been here. For some reason the roulette table is calling to him, so he goes over there and looks up at the neon display that lists the last twelve or fifteen numbers that have come up. Two college kids, one black and one white, are playing.

There's a lot of duplication in the numbers — 4 has come up twice, 11 twice, 17 and 19 have come up four times each, and so has 0. Steve watches the two guys finish their bets while the wheel is spinning. The ball chinks around and lands in something new, 26. Steve buys a hundred dollars' worth of five-dollar chips, twenty reds, and puts a couple of them on each of the repeating numbers. A couple on 26 too. He's won this way before.

"Red inside," the croupier calls out to the pit people as the dealer spins the wheel. Most players bet chips worth twenty-five cents or a dollar, so Steve's bet is big and must be announced. The dealer spins the ball in the direction opposite the wheel's motion, and after a few seconds calls out, "No more bets." The ball whines around and around, then falls into the center and bounces across the middle of the wheel, in and out of a couple of spaces, and settles, finally, in 17. At thirty-five to one, that's three hundred and fifty dollars. The dealer and croupier look at each other and to the pit boss, who shrugs. They count out three and a half stacks of red chips and push them across the table.

Steve collects the winnings and places the same bets again, except 26. He doesn't expect to win, and when the ball lands the next time, he doesn't. It's something in the 30s. But at least it isn't an all-lose, all-the-time night.

He pushes the chips across to "color up" — exchange them for a few of larger denominations — and is given three blacks and two greens. He drops those in his shirt pocket, tosses the last two reds to the dealer as a toke, and heads for the big slot machines on the opposite side of the casino.

Rick checks the chip racks of all the blackjack dealers, looking for a depleted one, which might mean the dealer has paid out heavy. He knows most of the dealers. He says hello, waves, smiles. They seem glad to see him.

The dealers he likes, as someone will later say to an investigator, he likes "because of their personalities." Because they're funny, they tell good jokes, they keep the game moving, and they don't emote too much. They seem to be genuinely rooting for him. Of course, their manual tells them to be nice to the players, try to remember their names, make them feel like regulars.

At the casinos, chips come color-coded. White is a dollar, red five, green twenty-five, black a hundred, purple five hundred, orange a thousand. Rick drops a green chip, a "quarter," in the last betting circle on Roxie's table. Roxie's short, about forty-five. He's played with her before and won. She pats the felt in front of him and says good luck, as most dealers do when you start with them.

Rick goes through his greens and half of his hundreds in a flash, then breaks a couple of hundred down into greens and some reds. He bets two reds and continues playing.

Roxie is complaining about the cards, saying she can't get them right. This is her way of being friendly. She makes an elaborate production of the shuffle each time it comes around. She's dealing two-deck pitch, which means she's got two decks of cards mixed together, and deals out of her hand instead of a plastic "shoe." The yellow cut card is two-thirds of the way into the double deck, and the cards below it aren't dealt.

People come and go at this table, playing a little bit, then leaving. There is one African American woman who's been sitting at the table with Rick the whole time. Otherwise the players have been transients. After an hour Rick is down about seven hundred dollars.

Steve walks up, raises his eyebrows to ask, "How're you doing?"

Rick frowns, shakes his head, says, "How about you?"

Steve makes a thumbs-up sign and then a little-bit sign, using his thumb and forefinger. Laughs. "I hit two thousand dollars on one of those dopey Satellite machines." He pauses, looks around, sees his brother waiting for the rest of the story. He shrugs. "And then I had plenty of gaming fun."

"*All* of it?" Rick says.

"No, not all of it. I still have two hundred. I'm two hundred up." He looks at Rick's meager stacks of chips. "Why don't you try another table?"

"Soon as I lose the rest of this," Rick says.

Minutes later Mary's there, with a bucket of dollar tokens, the fake coins from the slot machines. You have to change them at the cashier's cage to get real money. She sits in the chair next to Rick and asks how he's doing.

"Not so well."

She rattles her cup of coins nervously and nods, lights a cigarette. Casinos are smokers' last refuge.

She wants to get away, but she doesn't want to leave too abruptly. She fears Rick will think she's a jinx. If you play blackjack, especially when it's going particularly well or badly, every blip in the environment thrives with meaning. You think Alanis Morissette on the sound system is a jinx, that the wrong number of ice cubes in your glass brings bad luck. What's the wrong number? How many are there?

Mary stubs out her cigarette, watches the end of another

hand, which Rick loses, then points off in the direction of the slot machines.

"I'm going over here," she says.

Rick waves, doesn't look up.

Roxie has just come back. She's working on the cards again, shuffling hard. "I'll get them straight here in a minute," she says to Rick.

A couple of pit people lean on the side of the table. Rick's known to them. They've heard that he's writing a gambling novel, and they want to know what he's going to write about them. He tells them he'll say they were kind and they dealt him winners. They laugh at that.

After another half hour, Rick's finished with the thousand and has to go back to the cage. This time he gets fifteen hundred on a credit card. He asks the casino host to okay the casino's paying the hundred-and-ten-dollar charge for the cash advance — something casinos do for people who lose plenty.

The casino host says, "You go on back and play. I'll bring you the money," and Rick takes the fifteen hundred back to the table. He doesn't play yet; he sits for a minute and then says to Roxie, "I think I'll do the salon."

She smiles. "I know, I'm a mess. I'm way too hot."

The salon is at the far side of the casino, behind frosted Art Deco glass. There are tables with twenty-five-dollar minimums; two have fifty-dollar minimums. Once in a while, the minimum bet can be as high as five hundred dollars. The tables in the salon have fewer seats, and players are treated with special care.

A Chinese guy with ten thousand dollars in a chip carrier is playing at a table by himself. Rick sits down at another table with a dealer named Lollie, who has two other players, one with three hundred dollars and the other with about five thou-

sand. It's a pitch game. Rick waits until after the next shuffle —
etiquette: don't start playing in the middle of a shoe — and
puts out his quarter, starting slow. Lollie is friendly with the
five-thousand guy. They're old buds. He has a powerful smell
about him — he wears too much cologne — and has a heavy
beard and mustache like the guys who advertise beard trim-
mers on TV. He smokes all the time, drinking some kind of
highball. They're talking about a boating party.

The cards come and go, and pretty soon Rick has won a little
something. He bumps his bet up to fifty dollars and wins a few
at that size, then goes to a hundred and then two hundred. In
no time he's sitting on twenty-five hundred dollars, even for
the night. The cards feel right at Lollie's table. She's busting a
lot, much more than usual. Five Thousand is cleaning up as
well. The guy with the three hundred isn't, and when he
leaves, Rick waits to see if Five Thousand is going to play two
spots. When he doesn't, Rick plays the second spot. He wants
the same number of hands played, wants nothing to change at
the table. This new hand would have been the loser's, so he
goes there with the short money.

A small woman with rugged skin steps up to him out of
the pit, writing his name on a card, asking him how much he
brought to the table.

"Fifteen hundred," he says.

"You didn't buy it here?" she asks.

"Cage," he says.

After a couple of quick hands, Five Thousand is Eight Thousand. He's playing first base, the first position dealt to, the
dealer's left. Rick is playing third base, the dealer's extreme
right. The short hand is between them. Rick bets a quarter on
that hand and two-fifty on third. The cards come out. He gets
two face cards on his big hand, a thirteen on his little hand. He

hits the thirteen, gets a seven for twenty, stands on both. The dealer flips and has seventeen. Rick continues to play this way, shorting the middle hand but winning anyway, and pretty soon he's up to four thousand.

It's now a quarter to four in the morning. Steve appears and sits at the table between Rick and the other guy. "I've been playing two," Rick says. "Works fine."

"Okay if I play one?" Steve says.

"Don't care," Rick says.

Steve drops a quarter where Rick was playing his short hand. The cards come out — he wins. Rick wins. The next hand is dealt. They both win again. And again. They play on like this until Lollie's replaced by a gangly kid who says he's a graduate student in chemistry. The big-money guy leaves. By four-thirty Rick has fifty-five hundred dollars. Steve has won about fifteen hundred dollars at the table, but he's still down for the night.

Rick colors up his chips, getting ready to leave the table. "Where are you?" he says to Steve.

"Close," Steve says. "You?"

"Up three," Rick says. "I'm going to find Mary and take a break." He wanders out into the main casino and sees Mary in front of a Wild Cherry machine. She's surrounded by buckets of tokens. There are six buckets, each full of dollar tokens.

"Jesus Christ," Rick says. "What are you doing here?"

"I don't know," Mary says. "I just keep pulling and they keep coming."

He watches her hit two more jackpots, then asks if she's hungry.

"Food's bad," she says. "Besides, what do you think, I'm nuts? I'm playing here." She knuckles the machine.

He goes upstairs and gets a hamburger, eats it staring at his reflection in the black window that's supposed to overlook the Mississippi Sound. The restaurant is bright and smells of soap and cleaning solvent.

Downstairs, Steve continues to recover, betting fifty and a hundred a hand, once in a while two hundred. Two Vietnamese women are now playing at the table too, and the small, aggressive, sharply dressed one doesn't like the way the bigger, quiet one plays her cards. She's not at all reluctant to say so, either — she's doing a running critique, talking to the air, assumes agreement. The dealer deals, says nothing. The bigger woman is shapeless, wearing some kind of shift. Her play seems slightly irregular, but not much. She split fours against a four; or maybe she *didn't* split fours against a four. She's quiet, but getting angrier and angrier, until she's muttering about all the advice more or less nonstop. At this point the opinionated one, who looks like a fashion model, turns to Steve and says, sharply, "What do you think?"

What he thinks is that this argument of theirs is distracting and may be costing him money, and that he'd really rather she hadn't invited him into it. But saying that doesn't seem such a good idea, so he says, "I think everybody should just calm down." He says this while watching the dealer's cards, without looking at either woman. It satisfies no one.

He's within sight of having his money back. He has got within about a hundred dollars of even — which is three thousand dollars — and then lost back to being about five hundred down two or three times by now. Now he's about four hundred down. Losing everything trying to get the last hundred or two is familiar, but quitting within a couple hundred dollars of even is not among the acceptable responses. At the next shuffle, he stands up, stretches, and says, "Could you hold me two spots here? I'll be back." The dealer puts out two clear plastic circles — "lammers" — reserving his places.

Steve goes over to the high-ticket slots and watches the two or three people who are playing them. One guy is waiting for a payoff, sitting in front of a twenty-five-dollar Red White and Blue machine that shows a jackpot worth twenty-five hundred. "I put two in," he says. He means two thousand.

Steve looks around for a likely machine. A cocktail waitress he knows comes over with a glass. A little worn out but nice looking, with lots of dark hair, about thirty, has a kid. Her name is Roylynn. "How you doing tonight? Diet Coke?" she says, and offers it. "I saw you at blackjack, but then when I got back you weren't there." He takes the glass and sets it down, checks his pocket for chips to tip with, then gets a couple of dollar bills from his wallet instead. "Thanks," she says. "Did your brother leave? I saw him earlier."

"He went up to eat, I think," Steve says.

Roylynn nods and looks at the slot machines. "You doing any good tonight?"

"I'm not hopelessly lost," Steve says. "Yet."

She shakes her head. "That ten-dollar Double Diamond on the end," she says. "It's been hitting all night. All last night too."

"Hey, Roy," Steve says, "I really do love you, but your hunches . . ." He shakes his head, laughs. She shrugs her bare shoulders.

"So I'm due, then," she says. She pats the machine on the end as she walks away.

Steve goes over and sits down, gives it a hundred-dollar bill. On the first pull, two double diamonds appear in the first two windows, but the third one turns up empty, which is worth nothing. Still, the heart stops. He plays the machine for a while,

winning some, losing some, working it up to thirty-odd credits, or three hundred dollars, on small hits before it just dives
and he's back where he started, with ten ten-dollar credits. He
sits back for a minute and then plays the rest, two at a time. On
the second pull, the machine stops on two double diamonds
and a single bar — eighty credits, eight hundred dollars. "Was
that so hard?" he says to the machine. After he collects the
coins and exchanges the tokens for money at the main cage,
he goes back to his blackjack table. The fashion model is gone,
but the square-shouldered Vietnamese woman is still playing.

"She left," the woman says.

"Good," Steve says. "She had a lot of opinions, didn't she?"
The woman snorts toward the place at the table where the
model had sat. Still burning.

Steve makes a few small bets, but the slot machine has put
him ahead for the night and he doesn't have the will to play
anymore. He pushes his chips toward the dealer, asking her to
color them up.

"You leaving?" the Vietnamese woman says, sounding almost hurt.

"I got my money back," Steve says. "I got no nerves for
this."

"Oh," the woman says. "Okay. That's a good time."

Steve heads back to the cashier. On the way, he sees Roylynn
and stops her, lays a green chip on her tray. "I'd like a Diet
Coke," he says. "When you have a chance."

She says, "That Double Diamond, huh? Told you," and then
flashes away.

When Rick is through eating, he goes down to the blackjack
salon, sits at another table, pulling two five-hundred-dollar

chips out of his pocket to turn into some playing money. He's serene knowing that he can drop this thousand without having any unhappy effect, that it doesn't matter. He knows it's his money as soon as it crosses the table, but he also knows it's the casino's money until it leaves the building.

He plays at the table until almost six A.M., buying in twice more and losing eight thousand dollars. Just like that. The last three thousand goes on a single bet — fifteen hundred doubled on a ten against the dealer's twelve. Rick got his face card for twenty; the dealer got a nine.

"Always the big bets," Rick says as the dealer sweeps away the three grand.

"Seems that way, doesn't it?" the dealer says.

Rick's now fifty-five hundred down. He goes back to Lollie's table. There's a replacement dealer, Lou Ann, a young, plain woman in her late twenties, brown hair, glasses, a school-marmish look. By now there's no one else at the table. Steve has disappeared, and the guy from the boating party who was talking to Lollie has moved on. It's just Rick and this woman. She's a good dealer, fast, efficient, sure. He buys two thousand and starts betting hundreds. The cards seem to come to him, and soon he's betting two hands at once and winning. In half an hour he's got seven thousand in black chips stacked up, ten to a stack, seven stacks. They stretch out along the cushion of the table.

He's only five hundred dollars shy of his nut, so he begins to play cautiously, reducing his bets. Looking the length of the casino, he can see the six-thirty morning light outside. For some reason, the caution hurts his game, and he starts losing again.

He ups the bet, loses. Ups again, loses more. By seven, he's out of chips.

He goes back to the cage for another two thousand, returns to find Lollie back from her break. He kills some time going to the men's room, waiting for Lou Ann, the replacement dealer.

When Lou Ann gets back, he notices she's wearing a bracelet of black webbed cloth with the letters WWJD embroidered in it. He plays a few hands on his new chips — small hands, quarters and fifty-dollar bets. He asks her what's the bracelet, what's the WWJD stand for?

"What Would Jesus Do," Lou Ann says.

"Right," he says. "Why didn't I know that?"

He starts winning. In a few minutes, he's back up to forty-five hundred. He holds his own through Lollie's shift, and at ten after eight, after Lou Ann returns, he bets two thousand dollars, the table maximum, and gets an eleven, a hand you always double on. Lou Ann has a six showing. Things couldn't be better. The six means she'll have to take a hit, probably has sixteen. Her chances of busting are good. With eleven, Rick's set for any face.

He puts out another two thousand. He's now got four thousand bet and only five hundred left in front of him. He tells the dealer to wait a minute.

Steve has appeared. "Monkey," he says. "Big monkey. Joe Young." Monkey means face card. Rick nods and smiles, then slides behind the empty adjacent table until he's fully a table away. Ethel, the pit person, watches him curiously.

"Go ahead. Deal it," Rick says. "Face down, please."

Ethel comes over, stands right beside Rick, both of them looking across the empty table to the one where his cards are. Shenanigans of this kind are allowed when they don't disturb anybody and when you're betting four thousand dollars. Lou Ann looks to Ethel, who nods. Lou Ann slides Rick's hit card face down under the seven and the four. Hitting a double down, you get only one card.

Then Lou Ann turns her down card over: a two, so she's got eight total. She deals herself another card, a three. Now she's got eleven. She pauses there.

Rick's heart sinks. He shakes his head. He's completely lost confidence in his hand. He knows he's lost everything. She's got eleven and she's bound to turn up a face card, a ten, for twenty-one. He'll have a crappy six to go with his eleven.

Rick is now hiding behind Ethel, who is chubby, five and a half feet tall, a slight European accent. A nice woman. He has his hands on her shoulders. A table away, Lou Ann turns over her next card. It's a five; she now has sixteen and must hit it again.

Steve is standing at the table watching. Lou Ann looks to Ethel, who nods again — the dealer seems worried about Rick's being so far away from the table. She rolls the next card. Steve looks up with a smile, mostly in the eyes, and at the same time Ethel, who is standing right in front of Rick and is a good twelve feet away from the table, says quietly, "Too much. She's gone."

Rick can't read the cards from that distance, but Steve gave him that look, and Ethel said it, so he believes. He pecks Ethel on the back of her head, gives her hair a little kiss, then does a jump and returns to the table, where he watches Lou Ann count out his four thousand dollars' worth of winnings. She starts to count the money and Ethel waves. "Just cut it in," she says.

Lou Ann makes stacks of the same color and the same size alongside the stacks Rick bet. Two new stacks, twenty chips tall, all black, two thousand dollars each. Rick slides the chips back in front of him.

With eighty-five hundred, he's now a thousand short for the night. Twice, he counts out five hundred, slides it into the betting circle, wins two quick hands with twenties. Now he's even.

He says to Lou Ann, "You got one more?"

She says, "I don't know." She's clearly not eager for him to bet again. Not because she afraid he'll win, but because she's afraid he'll lose.

He takes five hundred off his stack and puts it in the betting circle, wins another hand, another twenty against a seventeen this time, pushes the winnings across the table to the dealer.

"For you guys," he says to Lou Ann.

She looks at Ethel, who nods. Lou Ann changes the blacks for greens and then drops those into the toke box attached to the right side of the table, striking the chips on the hard plastic before dropping them in. "Dropping five hundred for the dealers," she calls out.

Rick shoves everything into the center of the table and asks for color. She gives him nineteen purple five-hundred-dollar chips. He reaches for her hand as she puts the chips next to his betting circle, but she withdraws her hand before he can catch it.

"Thank you," he says, his heart pounding.

"My pleasure," she says.

He and Steve wander away from the table, smiling, waving at Lou Ann, Ethel, the other dealers. It's a ceremonial leave-taking.

"Are we good?" Rick says. "I hope we're good. You all right?"

"Up four hundred," Steve says. "Mary's on the dollars by the escalator."

Steve goes to clean up and Rick gets Mary and soon they are

on their way out of the casino to the cars. It's light out there, and hot, almost nine o'clock. Mary has won sixty dollars and Steve four hundred, and Rick has risked a small fortune and come away unbloodied. After some traffic in Gulfport, Highway 49 is quiet, nearly empty, and there's not much on the roadsides. It's fields and power lines and early morning sun. It's a big farm out there.

5

Table Games

THE DRIVES to and from the casino were lovely and rich with the intimacy of two brothers in adulthood; a rare thing, that intimacy, and we both knew it. Through the steamy nights we talked about lots of things — movies, writers, students who were doing interesting work, former students who might have done well publishing or finding jobs, English Department business, colleagues we liked or disliked, restaurants, computers, the Rockets, the Clintons — the usual.

There was a good deal of talk about family, but after their deaths, not so much about our parents. We talked about ourselves in childhood, about the family when we were growing up, about the house our father designed in 1939 and rebuilt year after year, a constant model of change and development. Remember this? Remember that? We talked about the objects in the house, the furniture, where it had come from, the various incarnations it had gone through (our father was no respecter of bloodlines; if he wanted to improve an Alvar Aalto chair, by God he improved it), trouble we had gotten into and out of, cars our parents had when we were teenagers, the two

Argentine girls, sisters, we had once dated. And we always circled back to the gambling, how tonight was going to be different, what mistakes we'd made last time down, some new plan we'd devised for minimizing our losses.

Before he died, a lot of the talk was about Father and his deteriorating health, what he'd said when we'd last spoken to him on the telephone, what he wanted, what we could or couldn't do for him, how much longer he'd be able to stay in his apartment, whether any of the half-dozen ailments he regularly reported called for immediate intervention, how to tell, what if anything was to be done. He was a difficult man, and he hadn't stopped being difficult because he was eighty-eight and infirm.

After he died, we talked about Don, or Pete, or Joan. While there was still money inherited from our father, we talked about investments, and in that oblique way we talked about him. For as long as we could remember, he was always thinking and talking about money, especially in the last thirty or so years of his life. It was a consuming and often painful preoccupation. For years we watched his fine numbers appear on paper, charting stocks, keeping elaborate calculations, devising obsessive budgets, and in general worrying compulsively over every arcane financial detail.

For all that, he was not a successful investor. The family joke was that he was a "contrarian indicator." Still, we remembered his dissertations on the niceties and perils of investing, which sometimes included weary exclamations about all the not-so-very-bright people — certain friends and acquaintances of his — who succeeded, made millions investing. Whether or not they were very bright might be considered immaterial, we had pointed out to him, in view of the fact that they *made* the millions. Well, if that was who we wanted to be, he'd say.

Everything has its price, he'd say. Now, en route to the casino, we would talk about investments, but since most of his money was stopping there, the talk didn't go far. Mostly we were trying on the investor's jacket while we busied ourselves buying chips.

We two brothers, together in adulthood as in childhood, depended on each other, enabled each other, even while we laughed at the word "enabled." Taking that seventy-mile drive from Hattiesburg to Gulfport, sometimes more than once a week, we talked with an easy friendliness and warmth we often could not quite achieve otherwise, without gambling as the common card between us. Even when we were losing, we knew our conversations were something of value, a feature of the addiction, and that in any system of values this one could clearly be marked as priceless.

This wide and easy talk on our gambling trips was what remained of the family. We were kids again, making a fort or throwing a football around in the backyard, building something in the bedroom with Lincoln Logs, playing with electric trains, making a movie with our father's long-unused eight-millimeter camera.

It was clear, even though we didn't talk about it, that there were connections between our gambling and the deaths of our parents. Probably there were many other reasons that had little to do with this loss, but even as we were doing it, the gambling didn't make sense to us without the disappearance of the family.

Maybe it was a ritual, the two of us together doing penance. For what, who knew? We didn't love our parents enough, we didn't help them enough, we were mean to our father, we withheld our love and affection, or we hadn't worked hard enough to find a way to deliver our love and affection in sufficient quantity, or we had failed to stop him from killing our mother. He had done that in some sense: badgered her to death, controlled her to death, drove her crazy with his craziness.

Perhaps gambling was a celebration of this togetherness, this partnership the two of us had, a partnership in the illicit, life-affirming, adrenaline-rich euphoria of gambling for more money than we could afford. Gambling right up to the expanding limits of our credit cards, gambling beyond our bank balances, gambling next month's rent, next month's mortgage payment, next month's car payment. And all for Father, or against Father; for Mother, or maybe against her. Look Ma, no hands.

A lot has been written about gambling addiction. We read some of it. Some made sense, some didn't. We didn't deny we were addicted, just as we had never denied addictions to cigarettes or alcohol years before. There seemed no point in denial. But both of us thought that an addiction was *just* an addiction, a set of circumstances, a habit that could be undone, rebuilt, fixed.

Within months of Peter's and Don's diagnoses of throat cancer in 1988, both of us quit smoking, discarding habits of twenty-five years. We thought we could quit gambling in the same way if we had to, and that we would when the moment was right. Ours was an addiction with a parachute, a happy ending. This was what we told ourselves on the highway heading south.

We knew a fair amount about blackjack — more, likely, than the average casino player. We'd been playing cards since we were kids, learning at the dining room table in the family house, playing with our mother and father and with our brothers and sister. We used to play for matches or toothpicks or chips, then nickels, dimes, and quarters.

Later, still in our teens, there were frequent family poker games. We told jokes, kidded and taunted each other, gloated and wept, played out hostilities and aggressions, and sometimes briefly held grudges. Our mother's play was sweet. Sometimes she'd try to give you your money back; our father was so serious and so good he almost always won. In fact, thinking back on it now, Father was true to his type. He was a heavyset but relatively short man, and he seemed to win at every game he played, be it poker or chess or Scrabble. As a small man, he made it his business to win.

The children, too, played in ways that illuminated their characters — careful, wild, knowing. Now, driving to the casinos as adults, we were not silly enough to blame our problems on these old family poker games, but certainly gambling was never on anyone's list of serious sins.

The family showed itself at those dinner-table poker games — a group turned inward, with the children relying on each other and their parents, and the parents relying on each other and their children. It was an us-and-them organization. "Us" was the family and everybody else was "them."

We were not exactly taught that people outside the family were stupid, vicious, venal, small, and out for themselves, but the message we sometimes got from our father wasn't far from that. There were those he admired and loved, his own father foremost, and others who had been his teachers, and certain architects and craftsmen he respected. He didn't fail to notice fine behavior. He liked people who cared about their work. Then there was that other, far larger group, the ones who cut corners. We heard that by and large people did what they did for the crudest, basest motives, and we had to be on the lookout for that. We were not taught that everyone else would cheat if given the chance, but we were taught that this happened in the world, that it was a danger. Our father was not well socialized. He had hard, demanding attitudes about other people, and yet one night in the upstairs office, when he was about seventy years old, he could say to Steve, wistfully, "You know what I really want? I'd like about five or six guys to play cards with."

Our mother was sure of herself and comfortable being who she was, but she was no social butterfly, either. Before she got quite old, she had a few close friends and would sometimes play bridge or take classes or go shopping with them, but she was always most comfortable at home.

When we drove down to Gulfport, we were being brothers in the best sense. Getting to that point was no mean accomplishment. It meant we had learned some things from our father, learned which things to keep and which to discard. It meant that what our mother taught us had not been lost.

Our mother was a sweetheart, so our memory of her was inclined to be generous, whereas our father was, among many other things, a bully. Our memory of him was inclined to be ungenerous. The teachings of our mother were well used in correcting the inclinations we had toward the memory of our father.

Since he was a child, Father had the nickname of Red, because of his hair and complexion. He wore glasses from a very early age, was apparently good in school, and was precocious to the extent that in high school in Galveston, in the thirties, he had slept with one of his teachers. Later, at the University of Pennsylvania, he studied architecture with Paul Philippe Cret. There he met our mother.

Father worked with Cret, Clarence Clark Zantzinger, and others before he went back to Galveston. One of his favorite stories was of a day early in his architecture studies at Penn when Cret was evaluating one of his first designs. Cret asked, "Where did you get this idea?" and Father replied, "Oh, I got it out of my head, Mr. Cret." Telling this story, Father, to imitate his teacher, would then assume a cartoonish French accent and say, very slowly, "Eez good zat it eez out."

He was an extraordinarily bright man who read a great deal and thought a great deal and even conjured some ideas about architecture that were way ahead of their time. Ideas for which he was never given credit and will never be given credit. He designed prizewinning schools and office buildings and taught architecture at the University of Houston and at Rice, where for a while in the early sixties he was dean of the School of Architecture. A decent man, but troubled and not at all accessible. A man of maniacally held principles with a few dark corners in his past. A man who talked to us plainly when we were children, presented simple rules and expected them to be followed, punished us when they weren't. At least he punished us unless our mother interceded on our behalf, which she often did, and in such cases he often backed down. He was that smart.

He and Mother made of the family and our early lives a lovely old-fashioned movie with snappy dialogue and surprising developments, high drama and low comedy, heroes and villains, wit and beauty and regret. Pretty much everything since then has been anticlimax.

In a way, blackjack was a movie too. It wasn't a good movie, but it was easy and quick, full of drama and jargon and icons — chips, tokes, and hundred-dollar bills — and fear, exhilaration, pressure. And the two of us, Rick and Steve, were in it together.

We played blackjack with different styles. The results were similar, but the processes were greatly dissimilar. Steve played cautiously, thoughtfully, with patience, marshaling his money, inching ahead or inching behind, fighting his way back from terrible losses over twelve, sixteen, eighteen hours. He might play from midnight until eight in the morning and lose four thousand dollars, and then play from eight that morning until two the following morning and win three thousand of it back. On a good night he might win a couple of thousand.

Rick played kamikaze style, betting small for a while, then jacking up the bets to five hundred dollars each. He'd get tired and impatient and toss everything he had in the betting circle — two thousand dollars on the table. He'd bet three thousand and double down to six thousand, all of it hanging on the turn of the next card. More often than not this loosey-goosey playing resulted in punishing losses.

When one of us fell far behind and started getting anxious and betting too aggressively, the other tried to counsel him, chill him out, slow him down. It never worked, but we tried anyway. One of the curiosities of this collective ceremony was that although we almost always went gambling together, we were rarely both down or both up at the same time, so the two of us were almost never ready to leave the casino together.

This made for some tense moments when one was down thousands and the other had just got even after a nightlong struggle. Once when Rick was up sixty-five hundred at first light, Steve was still down two grand. Rick had to wait, and while waiting naturally moseyed around the casino pushing bills into slot machines. After a time, he got interested in a particular twenty-five-dollar machine, and took a seat. Always a bad sign. Half an hour later, Steve came by to report he was close to even, but by then Rick had dropped five grand into the machine and was seething.

It's a terrible feeling to be far ahead and then start losing in a way that you just can't stop — an ineluctable fall, like gravity. It makes for a frenzied abandon. You don't care about money anymore. You want to lose it. You stuff cash into the slots as fast as it will go, and even as you're doing it you know it's hopeless. This is not the routine hopelessness of regular slot play; this is different, a unique despair, gambling with the recognition that you have no chance, that you will lose whatever you do. You persist in playing anyway. It happens at blackjack tables too: you throw money on a spot and make wild, silly bets, which, were they to come in, would make you whole again. But you know they're not coming in.

How do you know? That's also a puzzle. You begin to sense that, for all the mathematics, the calculations, the odds, the multiplying strategies of working the percentages, something else is at work, some loopy otherworldly thing. It seems built into the cards. There comes a point when you begin to think you know the cards before they're dealt. You've made a big bet, you're holding an eighteen and the dealer is showing an eight, and you think you've pushed, you're safe. Then you think, Unless she has an ace. No sooner have you had the second thought than you know she *has* the ace. You wish she didn't, but you know she does. And when she flips her down card there it is, the ace. And you lose again. Then you think that you *caused* her to have the ace by thinking it.

Do we believe all this? Sure we do, though not in the same way one believes mathematics. It doesn't do to spend a lot of time thinking about it, but it's out there, and when it's happening it is too real to disregard.

We were often at different tables, and sometimes during the early morning hours Rick would come to where Steve was playing and say, "I need a thousand, I have to double down." Steve would hand him chips or cash, whatever he had, and twenty minutes later Rick would return the loan. The next trip, Steve might walk over to the table where Rick was playing, doing well, and Rick would know in a glance that Steve was tapped out. Rick would take a stack of ten black chips and hand it over. A half hour later Steve might return and Rick would hand over another ten blacks and say, "Two thousand, right?" Sometimes these loans didn't come back right away. Rick might leave with Rie, or with our friend Mary Robison, or in a casino limousine at six or seven in the morning without having been repaid. Four o'clock the next afternoon, when Steve finally drove back to Hattiesburg, he would stop by Rick's place and, standing out on the porch, hand over twenty one-hundred-dollar bills. If his luck never turned, he might write a check.

Driving to the coast, we sometimes wondered why it was that if our mother's death had destroyed the family, our father's death, a year and four months later, was so horribly painful that we could not even shed a tear about it, that we could only box him up, put him in the shed, forget about him, them, everything.

Although after our mother's death in 1995 we started gambling in earnest, for larger money, toward the end of that year, having lost more than ninety thousand dollars between us, the gambling tailed off. During the first half of 1996, gambling was incidental to our lives. It had dropped off to a trickle — the occasional visit to the coast, occasional losses of a few hundred dollars. But after our father died in July 1996, an avalanche began. Between us, we lost more than seventy thousand dollars in two months. We had one rationale, which was that we'd inherited this money and we'd never had much before, so it didn't mean anything. We'd been gambling before, so why not just keep on gambling? Maybe we'd win something with the new stake. Maybe we just liked being there, in that movie, with those people, who were a little like the family we had once known, people we understood.

6

Gamblers

IT WAS NOT that we liked our fellow gamblers, the dealers, the pit and floor people, the cocktail waitresses. It was more that we loved them, at a respectable distance, the same distance at which one loves characters in books or on television shows. Some of them were interesting and some were funny and some were pretty. The gamblers were surprisingly good-natured, on the whole, with a few rude or angry exceptions, and those few served by their failings to point out what good fellows the rest of our companions were and what a good time we were all having.

One night a Hispanic couple joined an already crowded table where we were playing, the woman taking the last chair and the man standing just behind her, whispering urgent instructions in Spanish. Sometimes she would argue. She was sort of gorgeous. She bet her two green chips — fifty dollars — and won the first hand. She then bet her four greens and won the second hand, doubling her money again. She parleyed the two hundred into four, four into eight. By this point everyone else at the table was participating in her good fortune.

In fact, the rest of us were now in ecstasy, like in a basketball game when someone on your team strokes a shot from half court. Not that anybody said anything, mind you. There were tiny looks, glances, smiles. The woman, who might have been Cuban, had stopped betting her whole stake on every hand, but she was still betting heavily, and mostly she was winning.

Soon — it couldn't have been more than ten or fifteen minutes later — she had turned her fifty dollars into two thousand, all in green chips in front of her at the rim of the table. No one announced that, and no one stared. People typically stack chips in a recognizable way, and after a while you can reckon the amount at a glance. Two thousand dollars is ten stacks of greens, eight chips high, two hundred dollars in each; or two thousand-dollar stacks of black, ten high.

Now a transformation had come over the rest of the players at the table. There we all sat, participating vicariously. It was exactly what we had come to the casino for, this miraculous multiplication wherein fifty dollars becomes two thousand, wherein your risk returns fortyfold. If you sit in a casino for any period of time, at a gaming table or a slot machine, some stranger will always say, "A woman hit that one there for two grand last night. Then she hit it again for two more five minutes later." Or "Aren't you the guy who won five thousand on three-card poker?" If you're a regular player, among the dozens of times you've gone home thousands in the hole, maybe once or twice you *were* the guy.

But something else was going on at the time the Hispanic woman and her boyfriend topped two thousand. The ecstasy was drying up. There were six people sitting at the table: Rick and Steve, the woman, a middle-aged mother and her twenty-something daughter, and a young black guy wearing a leather hat. We all had the same thought at the same moment. You could see us straining, trying to communicate telepathically: *Run. Take the money. Get it out of the casino.*

There was perhaps a brief moment's hesitation in which the boyfriend and the beauty stared at the stacks that had miraculously appeared in front of them, as if wondering what they should do, as if there really were a possibility that they might scoop up their chips and hustle them over to one of the cashiers behind the long counter and take their money and go. But of course that did not happen. What happened was what everybody at the table knew was going to happen — even the Hispanic couple themselves, we suspect. They gave the money back. They bet it, bit by bit, until the eighty green chips were all back in the rack in front of the dealer. The beauty frowned at her friend, he looked at her and shrugged, she gave a tiny laugh and slipped off her chair, and they disappeared.

Another time, we were playing video poker, sitting in the middle of a row of machines. A Vietnamese guy and a chubby white woman sat on either side of us. They were playing when we arrived and had already struck up an acquaintance. They were now cajoling their machines and talking over our heads about the hands they were getting. Sometimes the woman would call the guy over to see what she'd got, or maybe to advise on a draw. It was clear that they had just met. One forms brief but intense relationships with utter strangers while gambling together, which is as intoxicating and as intimate as drinking together, although usually less messy.

Sometime during a half hour at the machines, as we punched the buttons and our fortunes bounced up and down in gentle swings, Steve placed a bet and turned up the following hand: ace, ten, jack, and queen, all hearts, and the seven of clubs. Four of the five cards needed for a royal flush, the best poker hand. With the Hold button above each of the four royal hearts carefully pushed and checked, we both looked at the seven about to be discarded. "King," Rick said, and Steve pushed the Draw button. The seven flashed away and the king of hearts appeared. The perfect conclusion.

The Vietnamese guy, whom we had forgotten about, knew instantly. "Royal flush!" he said, in the way one might say, "It's a girl!" or "He's alive!" He looked from us to the screen and back again. The screen itself was pretty excited, flashing the cards of the royal flush on and off in a sequence of its own devising. "Let me tell *her*," the guy said. He pointed to the chubby woman. It wasn't "Please let me tell her." It was "Stop. Don't do a thing until I tell her."

He waved for her attention, told her what had happened right beside her, on a machine she herself had probably been playing ten minutes earlier. The woman gave a slight smile, sighed, and returned to her machine more fiercely committed than ever.

The win was just two hundred and fifty dollars, but the money wasn't the point. The perfect thing had happened. The possibility of perfection was something most of our friends and colleagues at the university where we worked no longer believed in. They had grown up, become wise, accepted things as they were. But everybody in the casino believed. However crude, however dizzy, however self-deluded these people may have been, they knew how to hope, how to imagine life as something other than a dreary chore. They imagined that something wonderful might happen, something that could change their lives. This was their fool's secret, one they shared with drunks, artists, and children, all of whom they resembled.

We found that we understood these gamblers better than

we understood the men and women at the university, people who — full of purpose and high sentence and often considerable charm — seemed curiously reduced when it came to vision and possibility.

The English Department was a place of twenty-year turf wars and otherwise endearing behavior, of people who pressed long-time graduate students to call them "Santa" in the privacy of their offices, but please, please, "*Doctor* Claus" in the public halls. We had dear friends among these folks, but taken as a whole the atmosphere of the department was a shade dry, so we saved our best jokes for the students, who often got them and made better jokes of their own in return. Still, jokes themselves, which were the basis of our social training in the family, what there was of it, were not privileged in the academy. They were not reckoned as sufficiently serious.

Our fellow gamblers were serious, not like academics but in the furious way that children are serious, concentrating on play, oblivious, intense, yet at ease. Essentially they came to the casino to be children.

Gambling is a child's vice practiced largely by adults, often aging adults. Every day, beginning soon after eight in the morning, clouds of gray-haired people, in couples and in groups, arrived in buses that had brought them from the local airport or along the coast from Florida. We were often there to greet them. Many were sixty and seventy years of age. They came to play. Because money was involved, it was play with an extra edge, but it was still play, and they were still children. That was something we understood.

We were children. We weren't particularly proud of that, but we weren't ashamed of it either, and we had suffered enough boredom, done enough work, taken enough responsibility, and witnessed enough hypocrisy not to worry too much about it. Dimly but often, we began to notice that a lot of what passes for maturity, wisdom, or hard-bitten realism looks like play-acting. We can all pretend to be John Huston, but pretending to be his father, a much older and much younger man — well, that's a bigger project.

Our childishness may have had something to do with our own father, one of whose redeeming qualities was his intense curiosity, which he retained even in his eighties. He liked to think about things, focusing on ideas in a childlike way that left little room for feelings. He believed that if one just thought well enough, anything could be solved, ameliorated, fixed. By careful reasoning, Father thought, anyone could make a rich and happy life, overlooking the fact that it hadn't worked so well for him. I just haven't figured it out yet, he would have said. I'm still working on it. He was always working on something. He tried to allow for the disorder that emotions introduced into every situation, but his allegiance was to thinking, so frequently when Father started thinking, someone's feelings got flattened. This caused him no end of trouble with us, with all his family. For him, most situations eventually came down to, Well it *shouldn't* be. It isn't *reasonable*. In his way, he was a kind man whose kindness took the peculiar form of thinking for you as hard as he could, because thinking was one of the things he was good at.

He cared passionately about the things he did, and he was always doing things because he was an optimist and an idealist. The insistent hope, the sense of possibility, the idea that things could be better, could be made better if you tried hard enough, if you figured well enough, if you got another, better idea, if you just kept at it, was one of his abiding gifts to his sons, who customarily disguised their imbecilic idealism in irony, which they were not foolish enough to take seriously.

Irony was a kind of autopilot, a default setting. It was what lots of academics and others thought "smart" meant, but it was tiresome and so many were fond of it. They were so disheartening. Why weren't they better? It was the sort of thought our father might have had.

When you're sitting at a blackjack table with some guy with a Boston accent and a tenpenny common nail bent in half and hanging from his pierced ear, listening to him tell transcendently stupid snail jokes, it's a battle to believe that life is a dreary chore, designed that way by the Good Lord for some inexplicable reason. In fact, at that moment the world looks like a place of great tenderness and beauty. We liked this place of jokes and jackpots, preferred to think that a great new blackjack strategy or more fabulous run of cards would come. Each time we went to Gulfport, part of the ritual was "Here's the new plan," both serious and not, a hope and a joke at the same time. It was a problem, this tendency to think that good things were going to happen, that things would turn out well in the face of acres of evidence to the contrary. Father could never have anticipated that his faith that life really did make sense and his hope that by just keeping at it success could be won would eventually figure in our donation of so much of his well-preserved money to the casinos.

In this way we understood other gamblers too. They hoped as we hoped, they knew what we knew. They were always talking about what their husbands or wives were going to do to them (a wiry little drunk checks his watch at six A.M. and says, "She's a'ready thrown my clothes in the yard, but tha's a'right. I can change in the yard. I got to be at work at eight, and it's only a two-hour drive from here"), but they were always looking for an opportunity to celebrate, their good fortune or ours, it didn't matter, anybody on the team would do. We liked thinking of our fellow gamblers as a team, liked treating money — that bully — as if it were so many slim-jim paper towels, liked the fact that people don't lie much while gambling. A community of vice makes hypocrisy unnecessary.

If this was true of the gamblers, it was even more true of the people who worked at the casino. They were being paid to be nice to us, but they had no reason not to be, anyway. We were nice to them. We liked them. These relationships were similar to the ones people strike up with those who work in their doctor's office or supermarket; or the relationships our mother had for many years with other women whose children were the same ages as hers; or later, the acquaintances our father had with the maintenance men who came to do repairs on the apartment. Similar, except we were often at the casino eight or twelve or twenty-four hours at a time. Sometimes, after having dealt to us on a Thursday night, finished his shift, and gone home, a dealer would show up fresh on Friday night and, recognizing us with an almost imperceptible look of shock, recover, saying, "Not going well, I guess."

This is not to say that we really knew them or ever saw them anywhere but at the casino. We didn't. It was only that, at a distance, we understood what they said and they understood us, which was no small thing. Our relationships with them were like our relationships with Yancy Derringer and Jim Rockford and Kleist and Hamlet and Hakeem Olajuwon, about as superficial and about as dear.

The people we saw all the time weren't management, but

dealers and pit and floor personnel, waiters and waitresses, and cashiers. Some had come from Las Vegas or Atlantic City, but many were locals who had had other jobs and other lives before hiring on to work in the casinos. They were making more money now, and they liked the work better too.

Dealing blackjack or craps can't be any less dulling and repetitive than a lot of other work, and the glamour of the casinos is so thin you can scratch it away with a fingernail. Yet there's an element of carelessness and chance, instant by instant, card by card, roll by roll, that you don't find at the department store or the gas company or the elementary school. And a dealer is a performer, gets to talk while he or she works, make wisecracks, cluck at you like a chicken when you make some cowardly play, or tell jokes. They would tell us to go home when it was obvious we should, knowing it was unlikely we would. They had various styles, some startling — a stubby, prim-looking woman, asked by a player if he should split tens, might say, "If you had a twenty-inch dick, would you cut it in half?" — but the possibility of having a style at all is something most jobs don't offer. You got the sense that many of the dealers were people who themselves had a low tolerance for boredom and the narrow definition of proper behavior required in the nine-to-five jobs they had held before. Some of them were young, paying their way through college, but for others, working in a casino was a way to flee the dreariness of their previous work. They got to tell the truth, joke, play. We understood the appeal of all that, and we got the jokes, and after a while these people were, in a curious way, dear to us.

7

Dreamers

I N 1996 WE PLAYED almost exclusively at the Grand
Casino in Gulfport because it was closest to Hattiesburg, the
easiest and quickest drive. We hoped to win. It always
seemed as if you ought to be able to win. We didn't plan to
lose. We studied the odds of what games to play and what
games to avoid. We tried craps for a while, which is a good
casino game, but it seemed too chancy. All the books said the
odds were good — the odds were among the best — but when
you were throwing the dice or placing your bets while someone else was throwing the dice, it felt like betting on the toss of
a coin, and too often it went wrong.

Instead, we concentrated on blackjack, where players have
the best chance of an even game or, in some circumstances, a
slight advantage. We studied various methods of counting
cards. We bought books by Edward O. Thorp, Arnold Snyder,
Bryce Carlson, and a dozen other experts. Literally. We re-
searched the different card counts: the Red Seven count, the
standard Thorp count, the Zen count. We memorized tables of
figures for "basic strategy," a system for telling the player what
his play should be, based on his two cards and whatever card

the dealer has showing. This was a simple set of probabilities distilled into an even simpler action table you could print on something the size of a credit card. We did that. We made our own special blackjack cards, feathering together material from several books, making it easy to read and to follow. We put names on the backs of the cards, like "The Win While You Sleep Blackjack Strategy Card," and we put a copyright notice and a price and a "Made in the USA" stamp. Since these kinds of cards were routinely sold in casinos and in bookstores, drugstores, gas stations, and snoball stands, we even imagined we might be able to make a little money.

The problem with basic strategy was that it didn't work unless you were counting cards. If you counted cards using one of the systems, you could get a slight advantage over the house — a half percent, sometimes as much as one and a half percent. This meant you could make one and a half percent on your money — not on your stake but on the money you played — and because the average blackjack table goes through sixty to a hundred hands an hour, even if you're betting small you bet a lot of money over the course of a gambling session.

You could count cards and make money so long as the standard deviation didn't get you. We were no math wizards, but in several of the more conservative books the authors mentioned that the standard deviation in blackjack play was about four percent. We didn't quite know what standard deviation was, but figured it meant something like this: although with careful play and card counting we could gain a theoretical one-and-a-half-percent advantage over the house, there was also at work a four-percent swing in the probabilities. That is, the actual results in play could veer from the probable results by as much as four percent either way at any time. In the long term, the standard deviation wouldn't hurt you, but the long term was measured in millions of hands, more than we were likely to play in our lifetimes. As we understood it, that meant that even if you managed to get a one-and-a-half-percent advantage over the house long term by brilliant and perfect play, in the short term the standard deviation could wipe you out anyway.

On the other hand, we figured the standard deviation could work in our favor if we happened to be on the right side of it at any given moment. The whole business of counting cards was the antithesis of our motive in playing blackjack. It just wasn't much *fun* counting cards. It was hard work. You had to concentrate and watch everything with headachy eyes. It was impossible to count and still joke with the dealers and pit bosses, bet crazily, and generally have a high old time.

Card counting made playing more like a job, like solid-waste management. We already had jobs, so it didn't make sense to play blackjack that way. We took the time to learn basic strategy, but after that we played pretty much by ear. We counted cards sometimes, but in an ad hoc way, not a way the experts recommended. And we lost a lot of money. At first not so much, but then a lot, and then a lot more.

Neither of us worried much about losing. We drove to the coast, played all night, lost two or three or five thousand dollars, went home, taught our classes, made jokes about how horrible it had been, and waited for the next chance to go. In hindsight, this response — not being horrified — should have tipped us that something wicked was afoot.

We went home in the mornings and called our newfound brokers, the ones handling the accounts to which our father's funds had been distributed, and sold stocks and bonds to cover the night's losses. At the beginning there was plenty of money in the accounts and not so much money being lost, so it was easy to sell five thousand dollars' worth of bonds. It barely seemed to make an impact on our balances, which seemed damn high to us. Like a lot of people, we usually spent whatever we could get our hands on. Apart from our university retirement accounts, which we could not touch, neither of us had much in the way of liquid assets.

It felt okay, almost good, to switch the money around, move cash into local accounts from faraway accounts, knowing that money was covering the checks and markers that had been written the night before. It felt like high finance. If we got home before business hours on the East Coast, we might wait and make a few calls after eight A.M., tycoon style, move some money before going to bed and catching four or five hours of sleep before classes began that afternoon.

It might be good storytelling to say that these binges destroyed our ability to do our work at the university, but it wasn't so. If anything, we were more vigilant, more thorough. We carefully prepared our classes before we went gambling. We read the students' stories and essays, and our written responses were as thoughtful and comprehensive as always. We prepared to talk about the responses in class, and we prepared to talk again about the work in student conferences. Writing workshops are not courses for which you can pull out a tweed coat and some musty lecture you wrote in graduate school, down a jolt of caffeine, and Bob's your uncle. Some college teaching is assembly-line stuff, but creative writing is anything but. There is no way to fake it, no way to put the horn to your lips and *pretend* to play — there are no other horns to cover for you. Since we stayed up all night and slept mornings anyway, a habit for both of us since the seventies, not much changed when we stayed up all night at the casino. Maybe we got to bed a couple of hours later — maybe at eight instead of six — or sometimes Steve stayed over on days he didn't have classes to teach, but overall our schedules weren't significantly disturbed.

Having money to cover our losses made gambling and losing a whole lot easier, comfortable even. Some of our credit cards got jacked up pretty high. When we exceeded our lines of credit with the casino, we took money on credit cards, for which we paid extraordinary fees on the order of seventy dollars per thousand. We would get up to ten or fifteen thousand dollars on a card, pay it back down out of the investment money, then run it up again. Soon we were selling more of Father's bonds than we wanted to.

We were happy to have our father's money, money he had worked hard to save and keep, to cultivate, and we knew it was the only large sum we were ever likely to get for any reason, from anyone. Ours was not a family with hidden aunts or uncles who were terribly well-to-do and greatly fond of us. No mysterious Barthelmes lurking in foreign capitals all set to deliver a fortune to each. As the money flowed out, we knew it was irreplaceable.

After a while that felt bad, the money going out and never coming back. Even though we had control of it, it was still Father's money, held in separate accounts, which we talked about and treated as if he were still around, looking over our shoulders. As if we wanted to answer to him for its disposition.

We felt bad, but that didn't stop us. We never said, "Hey, let's don't do this. Let's do something else. Let's use the money wisely. We'll make the old man proud." We probably both thought that, but we never decided to *do* that. What we were doing would drive the old man crazy, and we knew it. We could almost imagine him hearing that Rick had lost twenty-two thousand dollars in one night. We could see him sitting in his desk chair in his home office, his elbow on the drafting table, his forehead in his hand, his eyes staring at the rug as if there, in that pattern, some answer sat.

In his college days, when he was a swashbuckler, he might have thought it funny, might have thought it *interesting*, what we were doing. Sometimes we remarked to each other that it would be good to have him with us, since he was easily the best gambler in the family. Of course, we had seen him only at family poker games, but there he was a champ. Who knew, maybe at the casino he would do as well. But he was not with us on our sprees, or if he was with us, he was there only in the hundred-dollar bills folded in half in our shirt pockets, in the token of his money, which was blessed with none of his shrewdness.

A hundred dollars is a lot of money. Think of it outside the casino and it translates into lots of things, lots of goods and services — shirts, dinners, hamburgers, movie tickets, tire repairs, shots for the dogs or cats, computer software, sets of bed sheets. A hundred dollars is still a fair amount of money in this world. But in the casino it was a single bill. In chips, it was one black. One. If you played quarters, four greens. Either way, the hundred looked damn small out there in the betting circle. It looked weak. As if it wanted friends, some other chips to play with. It looked as if it didn't have a chance in hell of anything but a quick dance into the dealer's rack.

When you had enough stacks of blacks, the idea that each one of them represented so much food, so much rent, so much car payment, escaped along with the rest of ordinary reality.

This was true whether you had chips or bills. Many times we walked around the casino with five, eight, even ten thousand dollars in hundreds stuffed in our pockets. When we had the money in our hands it wasn't ten thousand dollars, it was just playing time, time at the table or in front of the slots. You don't care about it as you would at home. You don't feed and nurture it.

When we had cash in our pockets the temptation to dump it into a slot machine was strong. The slot machine rewarded you right away, just for putting your money in. It made attractive binging noises as it counted the money into whatever unit you were playing — one-, ten-, twenty-five-dollar units. With each punch of the button you knew you could win a fortune. We had seen it happen. Maybe not a hundred times, but plenty of times. And even after months of play and months of losses, even after years of losses, we still thought we might win.

Rick once said we would walk out of the casino one morning and one of us would stick a five or a ten into a machine and punch the button and win a hundred thousand. That all the debits would be wiped out with a single sweep, a single roll, a single twirl of the reels. That was the way luck worked, he said. That was the way the world worked. Things would suddenly and inexplicably turn in our favor. A hurricane of money and love.

When Rick's landlord told him she'd hit twenty-five thousand on a slot, especially when that happened, it seemed that the same thing was bound to happen to one of us. Steve's wise old red-haired car mechanic said he had made sixty thousand on the slots the year before. We kept the faith and the money kept flying out of our pockets.

*

Eventually we began to figure gambling out: they take your money and you go home. All the people who worked the casinos seemed to know this already, and they were a little apologetic about it. They knew what was going to happen when you walked up to their tables. They were powerless to stop it.

We sometimes told each other about how difficult it must be to be a dealer — knowing the players, telling jokes, grinning and talking about your family, knowing your players were going to lose, that you were taking their money, not for yourself but for your employer, about whom you felt the same way somebody who worked at McDonald's felt about McDonald's. These jobs paid well enough once the tips were counted, and were comfortable enough, but they had downsides too.

For the bosses it was three-card monte in an Armani suit, and all the Armanis lived upstairs. But the dealers were downstairs with the losers, and being that close must have been hard. Their job, whether they liked it or not, was to fleece you. Now, that was a reasonable enough job for a guy who had made a career out of it — a carny worker or a flimflam man or a business guy whose job it was to swindle other business guys — but for these folks, fleecing was largely new. They weren't used to it. They had traded in Burger King hats or telephone operator headgear for a tux shirt and a red snap-on tie. They lived in small apartments with their spouses and children. They went to the malls on Saturday. We talked to them a lot to find out who they were, how they spent their time. A few of them gambled, the younger ones mostly, but not very many. Some said when they gambled they lost. A warning plainly lost on us.

Gambling was joy for us. We were stepping out of our mundane lives. We liked hanging out, talking to, laughing with the players, the dealers, and the strange, slightly unsavory types who worked the pits and managed the floor, the lifers in the casino business, even though their company cost us dearly. We liked masquerading as people who could afford to do what we were doing — gambling with this money and losing the way we were losing. As it happened, we *could* afford it, but only because our father was dead. As recompense, the whole experience took us into itself, created a new world, fresh, dangerous, and private, every time we went.

8

Slots

TWO THOUSAND DOLLARS BEHIND, Steve rests in a comped room, complete with Jacuzzi, then walks back into the casino near midnight. He's had one hour's sleep in two nights. On the down escalator to the blackjack tables, he floats in a suspended state, like a ghost, watching all the other people who seem to be there having a good time. It's like a step-framed film; they're moving in slow motion or something, x-ray vision. He wanders over to a slot machine that once, months before, hit five thousand dollars for him, and he puts a hundred dollars in and starts playing. The reels spin and the machine does it again: three red "sizzlin' sevens" with their backdrop lightning bolts fall into the three windows. It feels pleasantly terrifying. Better than drugs, if he remembers drugs accurately, which he probably doesn't, because that was a long time ago. He laughs. He checks the machine once more, touching the first window, the second, the third, to be absolutely certain that this has happened, then he hands an attendant his driver's license and goes looking for Melanie, his very occasional companion on these trips, because now, after forty-eight hours, they can leave.

Read almost any gambling book and, after a lengthy discussion of "random number generators" and a short history of the Bally Corporation, you will see this advice: "Slots are for suckers. Don't ever play slots." Then you'll see a second lengthy discussion, this one treating the "house edge," that laughably small percentage of each dollar, on average, the casino doesn't give you back, and pointing out that this edge is nine (or seven or five) percent on slot machines as against perhaps half a percent on a perfectly played game of blackjack. If this advice is absent, you have a bad gambling book; it might be a P.R. piece prepared at some casino's corporate headquarters, or one of those newsstand magazines whose fondest desire is to run such a P.R. piece, accompanied by a four-color, full-page paid advertisement.

Slots may be for chumps, but there are worse things to be. You could be someone who spends his time sifting out who's a chump and who isn't, a spiritual fraternity boy. You could do everything right, and be made gloriously happy thereby, but then, you wouldn't be in a casino.

We put nickels, quarters, and half dollars into the machines. We put in one-, five-, ten-, twenty-five-, and, a few times, for the sport, "to see what it feels like," hundred-dollar tokens. The cheaper slots are sometimes played with real coins, while the high-ticket slots are played with bills that the machine converts into tokens or credits. Put a hundred-dollar bill into a five-dollar slot and you have twenty credits; hit something and you might win fifty credits, or a hundred, or a thousand. A thousand credits on a five-dollar machine is five thousand dollars.

Sometimes you hit it. The first time might be at a twenty-five-cent draw-poker machine, betting five credits a hand, a dollar and a quarter. After being there for ten minutes or so, while you're pressing the worn and discolored buttons to make bets and other discolored buttons to hold cards and yet another button to make the draws, just casually you start thinking, in spite of all the common sense in the world, that this machine in front of you is a "good" machine, or maybe that it seems "hot," or even, after reading one of those P.R. pieces, that you have found that lost Atlantis of slot players, a "loose" machine. Sheer genius, that word.

"Loose," with all its implications of sin and imperfection and factory defect, its suggestion that the customarily tight mechanical fist holding all those coins deep inside the machine has been momentarily distracted, its hint that this son of a bitch is tired, worn out, relaxing into death, about to come completely unglued and just rain money, its threat that if you don't hurry, the management will discover this treasonous machine and fix — that is, *tighten* — it double-quick . . . well, someone dreamt that up. The word is a miracle, inspires awe.

Anyway, you've had a couple of flushes and a full house and some three-of-a-kinds, and your original twenty credits bought with a five-dollar bill is up to ninety-eight, and you're thinking maybe you've got a loose machine. That five dollars is now almost twenty-five dollars, and that's not much really, but you've been to the casino only a few times before, and it's not just twenty-five dollars, it's *ninety-eight credits*. So what happens now? You lose? No way. You're a beginner. You are just now contracting this disease. The next time you hit the dirty little lit-up Bet Five Credits button, the machine delivers a hand with two wild deuces and three low cards, so you hold the deuces and discard the others, punch Draw, and what shows up? Two more deuces. Four of a kind, deuces. Five of a kind, really, because they're wild, but on this machine four deuces is a bonus hand. It's not worth a few hundred credits; it's worth a thousand credits. A thousand.

You do the right thing: you hit the Cash Out button, and the quarters start clanking into the mailbox-size steel tray set below the video screen, and you start taking handfuls and tossing them into one of the big white plastic cups that are stacked around the rows of slots for this purpose. It's like those movie scenes in which people are throwing money into the air or running their hands through gold dust, letting it slip through their fingers back into the pile. It's a victory over money, the tyrant that has been pushing you around your whole life.

The quarters keep coming. And then they stop. But you are not paid off yet; the machine just ran out. It's exhausted. It needs a fill. You have broken the bank. A light on top of the machine goes on, and you start looking around for an attendant. Eventually she comes, looks, goes away, and then returns some time later lugging three chubby shrink-wrapped plastic bags of quarters, which she tears open and empties into the machine's hopper. She slams it closed, makes notations on a clipboard, says "Congratulations," and disappears.

In a room somewhere, somebody is thinking all this stuff up, choreographing it — the machine running out, the light on top, the jargon ("a fill"), just how to package the quarters, how the inside of the machine should look to the eager chump looking over the attendant's shoulder — you know all that, but it still works. You are stupid with joy. More quarters start clanging down into the tray. Eventually you have three full plastic buckets. You carry these to the "cage" to be turned into bills.

You're literally weaving around the machines, lights are glistening, everything's brighter than before. A thousand quarters is Publishers Clearing House. Uncle Scrooge. The Donald. Unbridled bliss. Free money, and an experience that seems foreordained, ultimate, perfect.

Two years later, at six-thirty in the morning, you will hit eight thousand dollars on a five-dollar slot machine. By that time, eight thousand dollars will be looking across the ledger at a figure ten times its size in the other column. You will stare at this machine, tired, quiet, and you will be . . . pleased.

Hitting a jackpot is ridiculous, a joke, sense in nonsense. When people hit jackpots, first they scream, then they laugh, then look around for someone else to laugh along. It's odd. You have just bet, say, ten dollars and got five thousand back — five hundred times your money. You just made two or three months' salary in a breath, so you laugh. It must be at least partly relief, but mostly you are laughing because this event is an echo of all that you know to be so but in your everyday life have set aside for the more efficient functioning of social, political, and economic systems and the greater psychological good of everybody. This money just fell on you and it makes no sense. It's as nonsensical as love or cancer.

It takes a while to get from the twenty-five-cent machine to the Slot Salon, where the five-, ten-, twenty-five-, and hundred-dollar machines are gathered like some East Egg picnic of folk in dandy white clothes. It's a progression. We started on quarter machines and in time were playing dollar machines and then we moved to five- and twenty-five-dollar machines. Rick made this whole progression in a couple of weeks; for Steve, it took longer. We play a little roulette, mini-baccarat, pai gow poker, some let it ride and hold 'em and craps, whatever the casino has to offer, but mostly it's slots and blackjack. Rick plays blackjack almost exclusively.

The high-ticket machines in the salon might look like people at a fashionable picnic, but the players do not. They're a grab bag. Once or twice a country music star with his name on his hat came to play at the little square island of twenty-five- and hundred-dollar machines and had himself roped off so he could play in peace — never mind that no one seemed to know he was famous until the velvet ropes went up. Even then, the only person who bothered him for an autograph was a cocktail waitress. "We're the people who buy his dumb records," she muttered afterward.

Another guy who played regularly came from Louisiana, someone said, and he always brought with him an enormous roll of hundred-dollar bills and three or four other people, one or two white guys and a very calm black man and his wry-looking wife, who played the machines in a desultory way while they attended Mr. Big. Sometimes they would just sit and smoke at a machine Mr. Big wasn't playing but might want to play later, or had played and intended coming back to.

There were a lot of women among the slot players — rich and poor, white, black, and Asian — more women than men, probably. Many gamblers look down on slot machines. It's partly a macho thing, because slots are favored by women, but it's also because the house edge is so high, because the machines are so simple and playing straight slots requires no skill at all. In contrast, table games require a belief in know-how, an expertise that is freely and sometimes loudly directed at players who hit hands when they shouldn't, or don't when they should, and are then held accountable for every evil turn the cards take thereafter.

This faith in know-how — based on books and laws of probability, diluted with savvy remarks by knowledgeable-looking people at some table you once played at ("First hand in the shoe is always the dealer's") — is not entirely illusory, but it's only part of the story. Playing the odds impeccably, one loses thousands. Splitting tens, one wins big. Sometimes. Nothing deserves one's faith more than the happy stupidity of luck. Which returns us to the much maligned but honest, honest slot machine. There's an essentialist argument for the simple slot: this is true gambling; place the bet, punch the button, win or lose. Repeat.

And it's mesmerizing. You're ready to leave and go look for your wife, find her sitting at a slot machine in a dark, smoky aisle several rows over. "Melanie," you say a little loudly, so as to be heard over the music of the machines, the bells ringing and horns tooting and quarters slapping down into the trays. She makes another bet, hits the button, spins the reels again. "Melanie," you say, still louder, a little closer to her ear, so close that you have to check whether it *is* Melanie, because if it isn't you're going to get arrested. Still nothing. She keeps playing the machine, winning, losing. You touch her shoulder, and she glances up in your direction, then quickly back at the machine in front of her, punches the Bet Max Coins button, and the wheels spin again. Finally, instead of out-and-out shouting, you get her attention by putting a hand between her and the buttons. Only then does she recognize you, with a slightly puzzled look, and return from wherever she has been. The same thing happens later, more often, a dozen times, in reverse: "We're going upstairs to dinner. You want to go?" she says. You wave at the air, oblivious.

Yes, only chumps play slot machines, but sometimes chumps make money. It comes as something of a shock that the machines really do pay off, and the shock tends to come when we start playing the expensive ones.

One night Rick feels bad because he has won and our friend Mary's along and she has lost, so they go over to the high-ticket slots and he takes out a hundred-dollar bill and sticks it in a twenty-five-dollar Wild Cherry machine. "We'll play this hundred for you," he says. She plays and right away wins two hundred and fifty dollars. She moves to cash out, but Rick shakes his head, so she goes on hitting buttons, pausing before each play, and nothing more happens for a while, until she has one credit left. On this last twenty-five-dollar pull, three wild cherries show up — five thousand dollars. Another time, Rick moseys over to where Steve is playing a five-dollar Double Diamond machine and sits on the next stool. Rick has lost a lot playing blackjack. He takes some of the five-dollar tokens that have collected in the tray of Steve's machine and starts idly dropping them into the machine in front of him. Steve has been at it for half an hour, an hour, all night maybe. Right away, Rick's machine tosses up three matching symbols that look like blue and white turtles. Four thousand dollars' worth.

Another time, Steve, playing a twenty-five-dollar Double Diamond machine, has hit a four-thousand-dollar jackpot, and one of the casino people has come with the W-2G form and a wad of hundreds to pay him. She gives him his four thousand, minus the state income tax they always deduct, and says, "We need you to play it off," meaning that he has to play the machine once more, so it won't be left showing a big jackpot, a common casino practice. This procedure is ostensibly intended to avoid frightening off potential players, but it also induces winners to keep at it and become losers again. Is it a plot? When you've just won four thousand dollars, you don't much care. Steve punches the button again, the wheels whirl around and around and settle, showing a Double Diamond, a red 7, and another Double Diamond. Oops. Eight thousand dollars, twelve for a total. He laughs and sits down.

These ridiculous moments tend to become the only ones we remember, so the recollection that one year Steve won $132,000 in slot machine jackpots and still lost money somehow decays in the mind. We remember the day and the minute when we won twelve thousand dollars in two pulls and forget the hours when nothing matching showed up in the little windows. We forget the time we were sitting at a machine, having won five thousand but lost half of it back, with the remaining twenty-five hundred-dollar bills in our hand, when one of us says to the other, "Whoa, let's rethink here." The winner, who still has fifty percent of his winnings, gets a real hard-eyed, made-for-TV-movie look on his face and says, "What's the point?" and feeds in the other twenty-odd bills as fast as they'll go. We forget what we know about pointlessness.

There is a perfect alignment or echo between our experience in gambling and our experience of the world, and it is in the big win — a slot machine jackpot or a successful thousand-dollar double down at the blackjack table — that this echo is most apparent. All the disorder, illogic, injustice, and pointlessness that we have spent our ordinary days ignoring and denying, pretending to see the same world our fellow citizens insist on seeing, trying to go along to get along, trying not to think too much about the implications, all of it flows forth in this confirmation of pointlessness — by luck. Yes, that is how it is, the funny blue thousand-dollar turtle-looking symbols say. And we laugh.

A gambler feels a powerful rush of vindication in winning, but it's not about beating the casino or the blackjack dealer or the slot machine, at least not principally. It's not even really about beating money. It's about beating *logic*. It's about chance confirming everything you knew but could make no place for in your life. Gambling is of course a very expensive way to beat reason. You can get pretty much the same thing by staying awake for a night and a day, or however long it takes you to get a little psychologically unhinged, destabilized, detached from whatever you believed the day before, and then staring at the cat, the dog, the stapler, the back of your hand, water. Most anything'll do it, once you've shed your silly confidence.

9

Thrall

WE HAD HEARD about gambling and addiction, about people who had lost their jobs, their houses, their cars, their families, their lives. We'd heard about people who got crosswise with a bookie or other unconventional lender. We had seen the gambling movies, Karel Reisz's *The Gambler*, Robert Altman's *California Split*. We had read Dostoyevsky's novella. We had read *Under the Volcano*, seen *The Lost Weekend* and *Days of Wine and Roses*. We wondered if that was us. Decided that it was.

We discussed addiction on those long drives down Highway 49. We were analytical about it, examined it in excruciating detail. We knew that your average psychologist would have said we were addicts in a minute. We knew the threatening jargon, that we were "enabling" each other, that we were a codependency case, and in the normal course of things, had we seen ourselves flying to the coast every four or five days for eighteen hours of blackjack and slot machines, we might have said we were addicts. But in the car headed down there this characterization seemed insufficient.

There was a catch: So what? Being an addict didn't mean

anything. One of the virtues of having gambling as your vice — as opposed to sex, drugs, or alcohol — was that the disadvantages were felt only at the bank. As long as you had the bankroll, these disadvantages were only superficial wounds. At worst, we were in an early stage of addiction, before the wounds amounted to much, and the customary assumption (which all of the movies, books, and hand-wringing newspaper articles made) that the later, catastrophic stages were inevitable was something we didn't buy. We doubted it. We had been trained to doubt the omnipotent sway of psychology.

Ours was not a family brought up on psychology. In our father's view, the great seething life of feelings could be a damn nuisance. Father had more than a teaspoon of the Frank Bunker Gilbreth about him. Although the family did recognize the psychological dimension, pragmatism — some kind of physical pragmatism — superseded psychology when explanations or remedies were wanted.

Being good sons of our father, we rode to the coast night after night, streaming through the sweltering Mississippi heat, clouds of grasshoppers popping off the highway like a plague of sparks, humidity as thick as gravy, and when we said to each other that we were addicts, when we talked about being addicts, it was a joke — a joke with a nasty twist, but still a joke. Later, after we became accused felons, we would call each other Lyle and Erik, with the idea that a joke needs a Menendezian edge.

You're a gambling addict, so what? Have you got money in the bank? Yes? Go on being an addict. A part of the pleasure was being able to go over the top, way over the top, without any of the mess or travail associated with doing drugs or becoming alcoholics or cheating on our wives, which is not to say the wives approved. They did not. But neither did they react the way they might have had we become enmeshed in other vices.

Sometimes, at first, they went with us. Later, not. But even then, during our long gambling nights, we would call in, advise our spouses how we were doing, how far ahead or behind we were, tell them that we loved them. And we did love them, somehow more fiercely when we were at the coast, when we were free to go to the coast. Something about the intensity of the experience of gambling, of risking the money, of risking loss, made the security and solidity of the home front much more important, much more sweet. More than that, it was a detachment, the anesthetic clarity with which you sometimes saw things in the middle of a drunk. Once Rick stood at the bank of telephones downstairs at the Grand, leaning his forehead against the chrome surface of a wall phone, standing there after hanging up from a conversation with Rie. They had exchanged I love yous and suddenly, after the call, he felt that love with crippling intensity.

An addict is someone who "surrenders" to something, the dictionary will tell you, "habitually or obsessively." Most people are at least a little addicted to something — work, food, exercise, sex, watching sports on television, cooking, reading, the stock market. Some people are addicted to washing their hands. Some people trim their hedges from dawn to dusk. Some people play too much golf. Almost anything can be the object of addiction.

Whatever his pleasure, an addict usually knows he is, or may be, an addict, but inside the warmth of his addiction, the label seems secondary, does not signify, as we like to say over at the college. It's like telling a horse he's a horse. Take President Clinton, for example. When he was involved in certain activities, he must have known he was addicted to something; he just didn't care. We felt just like the president. We didn't care. We supposed, in our conversations, both in Hattiesburg and en route to the coast, that when the time came we would bail. We knew that push would come to shove at some point, and at that point we would get out of the game.

Steve, wisely but very late in all of this, bought a house with some of his inheritance. Made a down payment, got a low mortgage, *invested* in a home. Buying houses didn't come easy to us, in part because the house in which we had grown up was as much a cultural declaration as a dwelling, embodying ideas about design always to be defended against Philistines. Since we had left that house, we had lived in more or less ordinary houses for many years, but we had always rented. Buying an undistinguished house seemed like giving in, disloyalty. There were other reasons, of course. We had led unstable lives, so the idea of settling in the same place for thirty years had seemed laughable. Until Steve started teaching, and for some time afterward, he had never had the steady income to envision buying a house. Buying a house seemed rash when half one's worldly goods were in cardboard boxes awaiting the next move.

We admitted having "addictive personalities," but we *liked* our addiction, the object of our addiction. It wasn't so different from all the other things, large and small, that we had intense attachments to — Diet Coke and Russian writers, springer spaniels and computers, box wrenches and movies. From childhood we had been taught that the object of an addiction was secondary. It was the way in which you cared about something, the quality of your interest rather than its object, that mattered. The first measure of the quality of an interest was its intensity, its thoroughgoingness. Best was to surrender oneself to something habitually or obsessively. We had done that all our lives.

Now the important thing was gambling. The care and feeding of our addiction, the pleasure of our addiction. Gambling was a very cerebral, almost slow-motion activity, which made it easy to savor. It was markedly more satisfying because we were doing it together. As brothers, we shared all the surprise and exhilaration of a new and consuming interest, like any new hobby — skydiving, methamphetamine. Codependency has its good side. Both doing it, we were each part performer and part audience. Every gambling session wrote its own swift, strange story, filled with highs and lows, finely calibrated details ("she flipped another five . . .") and compelling nuances ("and I thought, 'Fuck, ace, next one's an ace,' and then, sure as shit . . ."). Gamblers want to talk. For us, there was always someone to tell, someone who knew in his blood what you were talking about. After a trip, our conversations went on for days, full of lurid, taunting laughter. The kind that revealed just how completely we were hooked on risk, on gambling.

We weren't measuring ourselves against the real daredevils of the culture; we were measuring ourselves against other normal people, middle-class people, good solid stock, people with jobs, families, houses, cars, and responsibilities that they dispatched in a workmanlike way. People like us. We told ourselves that betting a thousand dollars on a hand of blackjack might be stupid, but it wasn't as stupid as shooting yourself full of heroin or, as various members of our family had done for years, drinking yourself into oblivion by five o'clock in the afternoon — or better yet, doing it by noon, waking up at three and doing it again by five, having dinner and doing it again by nine. Maybe we were just looking for a way to keep up with the rest of the family, members of which had had their troubles with various forms of conspicuous consumption, of obsession, of, well, for lack of a better word, addiction. Yes, it ran in the family. From our father on down, maybe even from *his* father on down.

The only time you really think of yourself as an addict is when you want to stop. When it's time to stop. When you're in so much trouble that stopping is the only thing left. But we never got there. We could afford it. It was fun. It was a way to blow off steam. It took us out of ourselves in a way that we hadn't been taken out of ourselves by anything else.

We had had good luck with addictions in the past. Both of us had been drinkers and smokers. Rick had been a drunk in his early twenties, but had stopped dead after he moved to New York and discovered that getting drunk and waking up at four A.M. on a Lower East Side street was not healthy. Steve had long since given up heavy drinking for steady drinking, three drinks a day, give or take a couple, for the past thirty years. Both of us had had smoking habits — two or three packs a day — and while we'd tried to curb them, following the path of declining tar and nicotine, going from regular cigarettes to pretend cigarettes like True and Carlton, we'd had no intention of quitting until, as mentioned, our two older brothers were diagnosed with throat cancer, one within a month of the other.

We quit smoking.

But gambling wasn't producing a downside for us. Gambling was only producing the release, the euphoria, and the opportunity to behave bizarrely, just like — we imagined — ordinary, everyday people. We didn't think we were wild and crazy; we thought gambling made us regular guys.

It was an aesthetic thing too. Everywhere around us were writers and artists and professors, hard at work at what Ishmael Reed describes as "all wearing the same funny hat." It had long seemed obvious that the best course was the other direction. Neither of us had the customary late-twentieth-century middle-class phobia for people who were deemed ordinary. In fact, ordinary was what we both liked best.

What we didn't like about the academy was the falseness: conservative people presenting themselves in Che Guevara suits, digging hard for career advantage while settling hearty congratulations all around for assigning radical authors to their students to read, thus threatening the established order. Soon they would take their SUVs into the mountains.

This put a little extra heat under the affection we had for the ordinary people we imagined existed somewhere and for whom we felt a special kinship. It was ordinariness that we were extending with our gambling, by being addicted to it, by doing it to excess, by risking more money than made any sense at all, by telling ourselves that we were going to win, or that we might win, when we knew as surely as anybody else that the likelihood of that was slim. Still, you'd be surprised at how much positive thinking goes on on the highway at midnight.

You'd be surprised by how dearly the heart holds the idea that tonight you might actually win, that this two thousand dollars, the last two thousand you have in your bank account, will be the basis of your big comeback. Even in the heat of battle, down five or fifteen thousand in a night, the not particularly well heeled but still liquid blackjack loser can imagine winning it all back in a flash.

And he would not imagine it had he not already done it once or twice or maybe more. Had he not experienced that thrill of the cards having run against him all night, run against him for five consecutive hours and having in that time lost an enormous amount of money, gone to the cashier's cage again and again, new resources, the thrill that comes when the cards turn, when they become your cards, when they became his cards, not the casino's, when in the space of forty-five minutes you recognize that you're going to win whatever you bet. And if you recognize it soon enough, and if you're secure enough in the recognition, you can turn around the whole night, turn around five thousand dollars in twenty minutes. You can turn around fifteen thousand dollars in an hour.

It's a rare, even amazing experience. It almost makes gambling worthwhile. Everything you touch turns to gold. You bet five hundred dollars and you bet a thousand. You double down and you win. Your stacks of chips grow. Pretty soon they are paying you in hundreds, then five hundreds — the purple chips. You've got a stack of those in front of you. Then, if the going is really good, they start paying you in orange — the thousand-dollar chips. The thousand-dollar chips are slightly larger, a sixteenth of an inch larger in diameter than all the other chips. You stack them separately.

Your stack grows, and maybe you bet one of them or two of them on a hand. Or you play two hands. And still you win. Sure, this isn't Monte Carlo, you're not some duke or some heiress, and so you're not betting hundreds of thousands of dollars a hand, but that fact makes your betting and your winning just that much sweeter, because you have no business in the world betting a thousand dollars on a hand of blackjack, and you know it. You have no business in the world betting five thousand dollars on a hand of blackjack, and you know it. So when you do, and when the cards are coming your way, and when your five thousand turns to ten, your ten to twenty, it's mesmerizing. Suddenly that business they always say about feeling like you'll live forever becomes a little bit true, because you've crossed over some line, gone into some other territory, become somebody else.

You're part of the table, part of the machine that plays blackjack, part of the casino, part of the system. Only you're not the part that gives your money to them anymore, you're not the part you usually play: the mark, the bozo. You've skidded out onto the ice in the middle of the Olympics in a huge stadium filled with cheering people and swaying, lime-colored spotlights and, suddenly, inexplicably, you can skate like an angel.

10

Money Plays

W E'D GONE FROM workaday English teachers to gambling junkies in a matter of a couple of years; that brought up questions of how and why and what, if anything, it meant. One of the fundamental things said about compulsive gambling is that it's not about the money. So what was it about for us?

We were adult children, overage children, who lost our parents and reacted with a clear disregard for the self, not to mention the other. Maybe it was about grief and relief and release, and maybe a newly visible aggression at having been held hostage for a lifetime.

Hostage to Mother and Father and to their picture of the world, notions of people, code of behavior, ethics and morality, their ideas about merit, work, and money, and finally, hostage to their affection. They were people born in 1907 who had used the lessons of their own youth to teach us how to live in a far different time. Father fancied himself as beset and bewildered by the less strong and less wise, a mildly messianic self-portrait, so that quarreling with his teachings made us feel like traitors and heretics. We were hostage, then, not only to their affection but also to *his* ethos and idealism, formed in the first quarter of the century.

Or perhaps the gambling fever was only a desperate and pathetic gesture of pampered children who had to face the absence of their beloved and devoted parents, their only family, the only group or community tie of substance that either of them had known.

Try still another explanation. Something simpler, something that has to do with gambling, that has to do with money. These two children — we two children — had not been schooled in finance. We were not prepared to make a great deal of money in the stock market or in business or anywhere else. And this being the case, did we perhaps imagine that we could use our (always highly regarded) intelligence to beat the casino at its own game? Is it possible we thought we could win in spite of how we knew the casino operated, about the casino's edge in every game, about the casino's percentage take overall, about how much money the casino was pulling in and the small portion it was delivering back to the state, and how much it was pocketing? Is it possible that we imagined we could win?

Now, years later, this is a terrifying thought. That we could have been so stunningly arrogant, so unspeakably naïve as to imagine that we might actually come out ahead. This is not pretty; this is "patsy" writ large. This is that of which one is born every minute. This is some kind of lesson in humility. But it's what every gambler imagines. And we were so *close*. Sometimes.

This should be clear. We don't think of ourselves as gamblers. We're pretend gamblers. This is an authenticity deal. We lack essence. We don't much believe in authenticity, although everyone else seems to. It's all the rage, no matter how dull the definition of authentic — fistfights and affairs with daddy. We don't think of ourselves as professors either, really, never did, even after fifteen or twenty years in the classroom. We worked at it, got great reviews, had students go on to glory, but "Professor Barthelme" makes both of us uneasy. We always imagined "professor" meant someone much more elegant and learned than ourselves; some of the people we knew at Hopkins had made a pretty good fit. But for us it was hard to think of ourselves as *anything*, looking out at the great sea of poseurs clumsily throwing cloaks about their shoulders. If we said, "We're gamblers, we're professors," we were speaking their language, not ours.

The money was not real either, but an idea, an abstraction, more so when it was in Treasury bonds in the computer of some brokerage house in Boston than when it was chips on the blackjack table. It got closer to being real when it was hundred-dollar bills in your pocket, even though it's harder to take a hundred-dollar bill as seriously as, say, a twenty. Part of the lure of gambling was its promise to make the money real, and it even did that, briefly, before snapping it away.

We wanted to win, we went and played and tried to win, we felt great when we did win, we felt lousy when we didn't. Of course, that's not the whole truth.

The second thing often said about chronic gamblers is that they love to lose. It assuages guilt, they say. What sort of guilt? The usual. See Freud on Dostoyevsky. Did we love to lose? That would overstate it. One would not want to place the weight of the losses on this small proposition, but certainly there is something about losing that is not entirely unpalatable. It satisfies the need for excitement, thrills. It's dangerous and it truly burns in a way not so readily available these days. So if not *love* to lose, then something else; we were at least *willing* to lose.

There are easy ways not to lose much. Play cautiously. Conserve your money. Minimize risk. Play the percentages. But above all, limit your bets. Simple. Over the years of our gambling binge we have often discussed mechanisms for limiting our losses. Great schemes were constructed, voiced, discussed, refined, set to be implemented.

Step one: Don't take any credit cards with you. Late at night, a brief ceremony: stand at the kitchen table and slip the cards out of your wallet into a tidy stack before you walk outside and get into the car. Step two: Take only cash money that you get out of the bank in Hattiesburg. Step three: Do not establish a line of credit with the casino, as much as they encourage you to do so. Step four: Take only one credit card on which you have a limited amount of money available. Step ten: Take two credit cards on which you have no money available. Step twenty-five: Only one of you takes a credit card. Step forty-five: Agree to limit your stake to five hundred dollars. Step one hundred: Agree to limit your stake to twenty-five hundred dollars.

And on and on. The list of strategies for minimizing our losses, for controlling our bets, was almost endless. Every week, every trip, a new strategy, a slight revision of the previous strategy. Steve would steal Rick's strategy; Rick would steal Steve's. We would play together. We would play apart. We wouldn't lend each other money. We would lend each other money. Rick agrees to leave when Steve says so. Steve agrees to leave when Rick says so. We agree to leave at a certain time, no matter what. Steve goes to the casino alone. Rick goes to the casino alone. Play only blackjack. Play only slots. Play only ten-dollar slots. Play only five-dollar slots. Play twenty-five-dollar blackjack. Play less, play more. Don't bet more than five hundred dollars. Don't bet more than a hundred dollars. Choose any one of a hundred betting schemes, Martingale and such. Walk into the place and bet it all on one hand. Read more books, study harder, practice more, memorize more, read the cards better, count better, play better. Get a simplified count. Watch the fives. Use the Red Seven count. Use the card counting system out of any one of the thirty-one books on blackjack in Rick's library.

Over and over, world without end, amen. The strategies usually lasted a half hour, sometimes an hour or two, after we hit the pushy maroon indoor-outdoor carpet, nodded in passing to the sullen security guard at his stand in front of the half-dozen glass doors, smelled the turbocharged air conditioning.

The thing is, with the card count, you can win. In fact, we know people who do. They have crazy eyes. Once, at breakfast in one of the casino restaurants, Steve met a guy who had been playing at the same tables, on and off, for two days. He made his living at blackjack, or so he said. "Think of it this way," he said. "The casino is like a bank. Sometimes they're holding the money, sometimes you're holding the money." There was a lot of "lore" like that, most of it equally oblique. But the guy obviously loved his career choice. He had mad eyes.

Card counting is not that difficult. It does require a great deal of discipline, a great deal of attention, a great deal of care. You sit or stand at the table — standing, it's easier — and you watch as cards go face up on the green baize, when players bust or when the cards are eventually shown at the end of the deal. Four, king, ten — minus one, you think. Deuce, jack — still minus one. And so on, ignoring everything but which cards have shown up. Later, you learn to pair cards and cross them out like numbers on opposite sides of an equation, skipping the paired cards and counting only the singles. When the deck favors you, increase your bets.

It's a simple matter of knowing when the deck has a lot of tens in it and when it doesn't. With a lot of tens, it's running in your favor. Ten-poor, it's running against you. You don't have to count every card, some don't matter — sevens, eights, nines. You don't count those. You count the tens, the face cards, the aces, the twos through sixes. You keep a running count, plus or minus, adding a point for each two through six, subtracting a point for each ten. That's it.

There are lots of variations. Some people drop the deuces out; some people add the aces; some people keep a side count of the aces; some people do curious machinations when sevens appear; some people give emphasis to the fives. All this works best on single-deck games, but not single-deck games dealt to the bottom. It works only slightly less well on double-deck games. It's also important to know how many cards are being cut off — that is, where the dealer inserts the yellow card into the deck indicating where to stop dealing and to start shuffling — how many cards are below that cut card and how many are going to be dealt out to the players.

You can see that it gets a little complicated, but it's not *that* complicated. It's not something you have to be a complete math genius to do, not something for which you have to have a photographic memory. But then here's the question: If it is about money, if it is about winning money, and if there is a relatively safe and proven way to accomplish that, why didn't we use it?

There are arguments here. Maybe we weren't convinced that doing this would win us the money. Of course, we never really tried it, so we wouldn't know, would we? Then there's the fact, mentioned earlier, that playing this way isn't much fun. It's work. Hard, dull, fatiguing work. To go whistling down to the coast in the middle of the night in order to work all night at the blackjack table didn't set the nerve endings atingle.

So it was only indirectly about money.

Here's where the word "win" comes into play. Winning is a big thing in our culture — a fist in the air an archetype, the late-twentieth-century American gesture. Winning is everything, many have said. In that word there is a magic release from the weight of all those nagging, dull concerns you're accustomed to carrying, a moment when you don't have to worry about it, whatever "it" is. You *won!* Winning is good. Couple the word "win" with the word "money" and you have a recipe for genuine thrills.

That word had a special resonance for us too, not because our family couldn't pay the rent or our father was always drinking up the dole, but because around our childhood home, money was a being, a spiritual presence. It wasn't materialism — no one was always buying or yearning for Cadillacs and fur coats — but money got a great deal of thought, seemingly endless discussion, a lot of air time. For Father, at least, it held the paralyzing fascination of a wound.

We're talking about two boys from a middle-class family with a work ethic and a belief in doing things well, not about the children of rich people. Had we come from lots of money, perhaps money would have nothing to do with it, nothing at all, but our parents were, to put it carefully, careful with money. They had a respect for it that sometimes seemed to border on awe. They had never really been poor, though Mother had been close enough, and they had both been through the Depression as young adults. As children we supplemented small allowances by making extra money working around the house, cleaning windows, collecting coat hangers and taking them to the dry cleaner, waxing the car. As teenagers we got summer jobs. We were teenagers in the late fifties, a time when frugal was good and saving a buck was earning a buck. For our father particularly, every dollar given to us was a chance to teach us something about life. Every dollar came with a lesson attached. The purpose of that lesson was to teach us to value *that* dollar, to think about that dollar.

Once in a great while Father would say, "Go get me my wallet from the bedroom," and when we brought it, overstuffed and worn, from where it was kept on a shelf in his closet, he would take out a twenty-dollar bill and hand it to us. "Go have some fun," he might say. It was a grand gesture, but a very self-conscious grand gesture. It left us impressed, grateful, and acutely aware of the money.

Father wasn't stingy. That's not the point. In our house the money was controlled by him, and he was captivated by it. This has always puzzled us, because he did not come from poor circumstances. His mother was a schoolteacher; his father owned a successful lumberyard. Still, our father held the dollar in high esteem. Later, when we had left his house, when we had the psychological leisure to think about it, it was clear that this high esteem had given money the power to beat him to a pulp, which it did, year after year.

Maybe our gambling was about that, or about friends, arrogance, abstraction, and risk. About ambivalence, careers, business as usual, and about being saddled with a role we sometimes didn't love enough. About money, too, and surely about our parents and their deaths, about our family, and about a world that didn't quite exist but that we could almost imagine.

11

Courting Loss

THE MONEY WE DROPPED gambling totaled more than a quarter million dollars. When we figured this out, we liked to say "a quarter million dollars" because it made what we had done seem a little bit breathtaking, especially considering who we were, what we were, what we earned. A little bit breathtaking, that was it exactly. We even amazed ourselves, or maybe we *only* amazed ourselves. Some substantial thing had happened, some big thing. Our otherwise ordinary lives had been interrupted to bring you this special bulletin: *Brothers Lose Quarter Million.*

A quarter million dollars isn't what it once was. Middle-class folks process a quarter million dollars every few years. At the poverty level, folks go through that much several times in a lifetime, and at fifty thousand a year you make it in five. For rich people it's a sneeze. A moderate home mortgage is going to cost a quarter million, or thereabouts, once it's done. And a lot of houses *start* at a quarter million. Sending a couple of kids through college can come close. Some cars cost a quarter million (of course, they're built for basketball players and computer hotshots). But it still sounds like a lot of money to us.

With the word "million" in it, it's an accomplishment to have lost it.

That second commonplace about gambling, after it's not about the money, is that gamblers want to lose. Losing is exciting, seductive, redemptive.

There's the phrase "born loser." There are all those boxers who seem always to lose. All those football and baseball teams. All those swimmers, race car drivers, and actors. The world seems full of runners-up, honorable mentions, places and shows. There are Formula-1 drivers who race for years and never win a single race, never place or show, never win a championship point. The same is true of Indy drivers, NAS-CAR drivers, dogsledding, footracing, book writing, basketball. Some people never win.

Yes, it's carried to extremes at casinos, where most people never win, but at the casino people don't take the game seriously. Almost no one plays cautiously, almost no one thinks he or she will win. They've come for the carnival, the sideshow, come to see the Smallest Woman in the World, or the Smallest Woman in the Whole Wide World. They're throwing three lightweight simulated baseballs at three painted and bottom-heavy Coke bottles. They're trying to drop a Ping-Pong ball into a brandy snifter from ten feet. They don't expect to be able to do it. They don't even really care if they do it or not. The point is to try, give the guy the money, get your ticket, and take your shot.

But that's not the kind of losing we're talking about here, because we were more serious, more ardent in our courtship of loss. We practiced, we tried harder, we dumped the cash our father had worked so hard to put together for us. Was the message clear? Was it, "We don't want your money"? Was it, "If we can't have you, we don't want your money"? Or was it, "Consider yourself repudiated"? Or was it more like, "Thanks for this chance to feel what it's like to be a loser on a large scale"? Or, "This money is a poor substitute for you"?

There are simpler things to consider: what it feels like to lose money at a blackjack table. You go down to the casino, write a check for five thousand dollars, buy that much in chips. If left to the discretion of the dealer and the pit, you'll get mostly blacks, maybe five hundred in greens.

You have the five thousand in front of you and start betting two or three hundred dollars on one or two hands. Remember, you're not well-to-do. Having five thousand dollars in front of you on a table is not your custom. That kind of money comes up only when you deal with down payments on cars, house repairs, hospital bills.

What goes on at the blackjack table is like therapy. The play is your therapy. The dealer is the therapist. You bet your money, take your cards, and do the best you can. The way we played, which was not smart, had a great deal to do with our lively imaginations. We imagined we might win. We imagined we might get cards that were very unlikely to come. We imagined the dealer might break or go over twenty-one, thus losing his hand and making us winners. We imagined all sorts of things. Steve was methodical, trying to play the flow of the cards, starting small and gradually raising his bets if he started winning. Rick was a lunger, making sudden tenfold increases in the size of his bets, following hunches, intuition, or magic. Both of us were known in the casino as erratic players, not exactly bad players, but surely losers.

So you're playing the game with your five thousand dollars, and you run through a couple of hands where you bet big, double down on an eleven, double against a six, whatever. You lose. After a while you're out of chips, and it's easy to ask the pit boss for another five thousand marker, which makes him happy. Now you've got a fresh start. You've got fresh stacks of twenty-five-dollar chips and hundred-dollar chips in front of you. You have what it takes to get back on your feet, which is money. You've got the chance to win your first five thousand back.

More often than not, this is where we found ourselves. We'd go to the casino, we'd start playing, we'd lose, we'd get more money to try to get back the money we'd lost, and that was the game we'd win or lose — that is, even if we won, which we did a surprising number of times, we would just come out even.

Money moves quickly. It *seems* very slow sometimes when you're playing, it seems as if everything is done in slow motion, especially when the big hands are played. With a twenty-five-hundred-dollar bet riding, the time it takes the dealer to complete the initial outlay of cards around the table can seem eternal. You've got your arms folded. You're waiting to get to the part of the hand where you take hits or tuck your cards face down under the stack of chips you've bet. Later, in the same game, you're waiting for other players to finish their play, to take their hits, to tuck their hands, and then you're waiting for the dealer to turn over her down card and to play it, hitting if below seventeen, standing if it's seventeen or above.

The deal feels as if it is on film: the action is going along normally and then the projector slows down and the image, the movement, starts to flicker onscreen. Every gesture is half speed, quarter speed, eighth speed. The dealer's hands — many wear lots of rings and bracelets, and the women paint, polish, and trick up their nails with inlaid stars and such — move across your field of view like spirits. Blood rushes to your head, a sensation like a sudden rise in pressure. Your head is going to explode. It's unpleasant but extraordinary. You wait and wait for the cards.

If the cards go your way, there is a sudden decompression, that striking *yes!* that has become the fundamental, international gesture of success. All the pressure in your head has dissipated, and you stand back from the table, draw a deep breath, wait for the dealer to match your chips in kind. Even then you're not sure you can trust yourself to sweep your winnings out of the betting circle and back into your stacks.

If the cards run against you and you lose, the blood that's in your head seems to fan out of your skull. All the heat you felt inside rushes to the surface of your skull, then it slowly sizzles away as you realize the size of your loss, as you go through the process of accepting that loss and preparing for the next bet, the next attempt, the next risk you're willing to take, the next loss you're willing to endure.

Early on, you notice that winning and losing are not so different. Both involve this huge buildup of pressure; the higher the stakes, the greater the pressure, the more intense the experience. This is one of the reasons you end up betting two or four thousand dollars at a throw, because whether you win or lose, you still have 85 percent of the experience, you still get 90 percent of the thrill. The losing part is not fun, exactly. In fact, fun doesn't come into it, but the heat, the dizzying adrenal rush, is much the same whether the chips come back to you or go in the dealer's rack. It's something you can understand only by playing. Otherwise, you're trying to know what's so great about chocolate when you've never had any. Gamblers know, because they've experienced it time and time again. It goes so much against common sense that it stays a secret. Even if you see it in the movies or read about it in a book or get told by a friend, you won't believe it. But play the game, any game, for significant stakes and you'll know. It's not whether you win or lose, it's that you *play.*

After Rick had taken some serious losses, he decided not to go to the casino as often, so Steve went alone. Once he came back and told Rick that the dealers had asked after him. Rick said he was glad to hear that and wanted to know what they had to say. One dealer had said, "You know, your brother is about the best loser I've ever seen."

If you're skeptical about winning and losing being so similar, take this test. Go to your nearest casino with a thousand dollars and buy ten black chips. Put the thousand in the betting circle at a blackjack table. Do this early, so the chips can sit out there as the dealer shuffles the cards or hands them around to be cut. Await your fate. When it comes, whatever it is, smile as it is being executed. Ask the dealer to go slowly. Tell her you're new at this. If you win, leave the chips there, stacked in the betting circle, and await the next round of cards. Repeat this until you lose. When you lose everything, move away from the table and dwell on what has happened. Don't be content with telling yourself how stupid you are. Don't be satisfied with calling yourself names. Don't simply conclude that you were insane to follow these instructions, to take this test. Instead, dwell on how it *felt.* Go over it and over it in your head, recalling every detail. Remember your breathing, the barely perceptible electricity vibrating in your hands, the twist in your neck and shoulders. Remember the current flowing through your body as you watched each card show, every anticipation, every bit of impatience, the little anger you felt about how slowly the dealer was proceeding, what you felt about the other players at the table, how your heartbreak rested on the fall of a card.

The family portrait. A staple at the Barthelme house. This from 1952.
Don, back from Korea, is with his first wife, Marilyn.

Mother on the beach in Atlantic City,
c. 1926.

Father, probably Galveston, maybe
Philadelphia, around the time he and
Mother met, c. 1927.

Rick, Pete, Don (by snowman) in 1949. The nine-foot sliding doors completely opened the house to the outside. The oldest child at home got the bedroom on the roof.

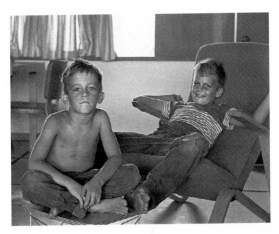

Steve and Rick in 1954. The interior was a hothouse of contemporary furniture, but it got no special treatment.

When Father designed the Hall of State building at the Texas State Fair, Dallas, 1940, he had the names of Texas heroes chiseled across the fascia of the building so the first letters of their names spelled "BARTHELME."

Mother and Steve in 1948. Behind her, the garage, Father's Lincoln Zephyr, and the house before it was covered with copper.

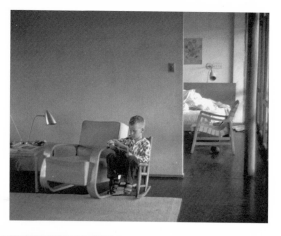

Rick reading in the living room, c. 1948. The missing master bedroom door caused trouble with the builder and the loan officer, but Father insisted and prevailed. There's a screen behind the wall for those non-architectural moments.

Steve and Rick playing chess, c. 1954.

Mr. Bart (Father's father) with Mother and Pete on the porch at his Galveston home, c. 1954. Steve and Rick have other interests.

Mother and the five children in the surf at Stewart Beach in Galveston, 1950. We went to Galveston frequently to visit Father's parents.

11 Wynden Drive, c. 1957. Father changed the house constantly, thought nothing of tearing up the floor or living with a tarpaulin as an exterior wall while he gathered the money, or the inspiration, to replace the one he'd ripped out.

The house in well-practiced disrepair, c. 1947.

Father with camera in 1950. We grew up being photographed mercilessly.

Steve in the playroom, Christmas 1954.

Mother and Father, 1956. They played Scrabble together well into their eighties.

The house (c. 1950) was an oddity on the Texas grasslands when it was built in 1939.

Steve and Don discuss a story manuscript, c. 1968.

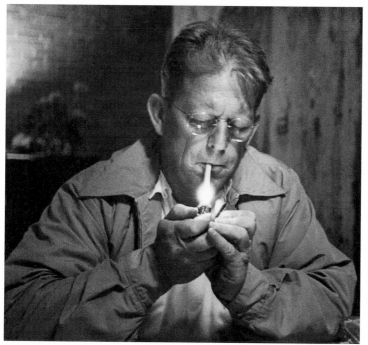

Father studies the problem of what to do with the wall behind him. Often the house was ripped up for months at a time.

Steve, Pete, and Rick in typical fifties gear, eating those pot pies, c. 1953.

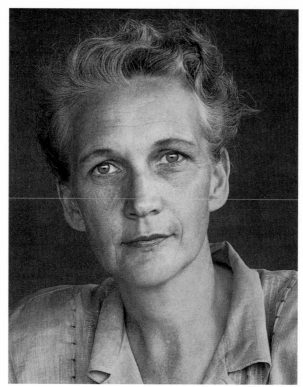

A favorite picture of Mother, on the terrace in the Texas heat, c. 1952.

Earliest interior of the house, c. 1940.

Father with Rick and Steve, c. 1953. Talking to the kids was a lifelong habit, something he cultivated. Often it was instruction, not empathy, but there was no shortage of talk.

Think of the chips you had on the table, think about what else you could have done with that money, think of giving that money to your spouse or your child or a friend in need, think about giving it to some charitable organization, think of giving it to a guy standing on the side of the road with a sign around his neck that says Will Work for Food, think about how afraid you were, if you were afraid, while you were playing, think about how much you wanted to get out of playing the hand you finally lost on, or how much you thought it was going to be a sure thing and you would get out of the game after winning it. Try to remember why you were there playing that game in the first place. Try to figure how you let yourself be so foolish, how you took leave of your senses, how you got into this thing. And most of all, once it's done, gently close your eyes, fade back, and feel it.

This last will prove the point. It's not unlike "It is better to give than to receive." It is as good to lose as to win. There is only a shadow of difference between them, and that shadow is insignificant. Winning is better than losing, but neither one is the goal of gambling, which is *playing*. Losing never feels like the worst part of gambling. Quitting often does.

III

12

Eighty-sixed

THREE DEALERS named Cindy were working the graveyard shift at the Grand Casino in Gulfport on November 11, 1996 — one a short blond woman, one a redheaded
woman who had a penchant for doing her nails in custom car
colors, and a heavyset woman in her mid-thirties from New
Jersey whom some people down there called Big Cindy. There
were other dealers we liked to play with, but this particular
night we played mostly with the third Cindy. It was happen-
stance — she was there and dealing. She was a sarcastic, quick,
wry woman who made up new lyrics to the saccharine pop
music piped into the casino and sang along — "What if God
were a Greyhound bus, would he run over all of us . . ." She
gave the impression of being a casino pro, someone who always knew what she was doing, who had it all under control,
an impression that we took at face value. We never met her or
any other dealers outside the casino, never talked to them save
across the blackjack table or on the casino floor. At the blackjack table Cindy moved the game quickly. She sussed out our
likes and dislikes, the peculiarities of our play, and blended

them into her way of dealing. She was good at the casino's assigned task of making regulars out of the players.

We lost close to ten thousand dollars overnight, playing mostly at her table, occasionally with her relief person or at another table when Cindy was off on her break. Dealers work forty minutes on, twenty off, and when your dealer leaves, you sometimes try other tables to see how the cards are running. That night Steve had wandered around playing blackjack, fighting slot machines, eventually joining Rick at Cindy's table.

Some odd things had happened, although at the time we didn't know they were all that odd. A uniformed security guy, a guy we recognized, spent some time standing behind us while we played. At one point he stepped forward, smiled, and asked Steve, "How'd you come out the other night?"

"Last week?" Steve said. "I did okay. I only lost seven hundred."

Later that morning, when Rick asked for a courtesy loan of five hundred dollars to double down — a casino custom, done to save slowing the game — the pit boss refused, unusual because they'd never refused him before. The shift manager, a thin young woman with brittle blond hair and coarse skin, whom we also knew, seemed nervous, but then, she always seemed nervous.

Just before Cindy's shift ended at ten in the morning, with Rick down nine thousand dollars and Steve down about eight hundred, three plainclothes security people, a uniformed guard, and the nervous shift manager walked up behind Steve at the table and said, "Are these your chips?"

Steve said, "Yes, why?"

The guard said, "Pick up the chips and come with us."

Rick, who had been looking for the shift manager to complain about the refusal of the courtesy loan, returned to the table. "What's all this?" he said.

One of the security men said, "Are you playing at this table?"

"Yeah. Why?"

"Those your chips?" he said, pointing to the two stacks of ten blacks in front of Rick.

"Yes," Rick said impatiently. "Those are my chips."

"Get the chips and come with us."

We exchanged glances, then did as we were told. The security person, the uniformed guard, and the shift manager marched us through the casino, making what seemed to us a humiliating and embarrassing scene. They walked us to the cashier's cage and told us to turn over the chips we had, refusing to give us money for them, instead forcing us to pay off markers the casino was holding from a prior trip. As the cashier did the paperwork, we noticed that the shift manager was shaking.

The whole performance was surreal — we'd been regulars at the casino for a year or more, were well known there, had lost a lot of money there, and they knew that. So why were they rousting us? We didn't know. We were fatigued, out of it, wondering what was going on. Ugly scenes from movies skipped through our heads. All the casino staff's usual chummy behavior, all the sweet grease that the employees ordinarily used to keep us content and gambling at their tables, disappeared in an instant.

"Let's go," one of them said.

"Go where?" Rick said.

The guy looked at Rick. "Just come with us," he said.

Rick asked the shift manager what was happening but she waved him away without an answer, and then three of the security people, including the uniform, walked us out of the casino and into a small, windowless, concrete-walled room hidden in the side of the four-story parking garage. There were a couple of cheap office desks, a couple of filing cabinets, a few folding chairs. We were instructed to take seats and then were cross-examined by the two sweaty security guys who had stayed with us all the way. One guy was big and meaty looking, the other was younger, thin, and stayed in the background. We sat there exhausted and bewildered, having played blackjack for fourteen hours.

They insinuated that we were having sexual affairs, both individually and severally, with Cindy, the dealer we'd played with much of the night. Accused us of meeting her at her house to plan a conspiracy against the casino. Their sneering questions weren't actually questions, but assertions pretending to be questions. We tried to explain we didn't know Cindy from Adam, but our protests were brushed aside. It was like being back in a high school parking lot, where bristling accusations and jeering sarcasm ("I think you know what I mean") were the order of the day. They accused us of giving and getting signals, told us they had it all in living color on videotape. They wanted us to say that we'd cheated. We hadn't, so we couldn't.

They seemed blunt and menacing, and the threat of violence seemed to float in the air of this steel-doored concrete cell. It was intimidation, and it was working. The big guy did the talking while the other one stood behind us somewhere. Every once in a while one of us would glance at him, not sure what he was there for.

On instructions from the big guy, the other one brought out a dinky Polaroid and snapped our pictures. Then they took our driver's licenses and copied the information off them, flipping them back across the desk when they were done. Finally the big guy tired of this and told us he was going to let us go. He said he *could* call the police, have us taken into custody, but he wasn't going to do that. He told us we were being eighty-sixed and that if we ever came back to the Grand we'd be arrested on sight.

The big guy turned to Steve. "You ain't sayin' much," he said, triumphant, as if that in itself were damning evidence.

Steve looked at the guy and shrugged. He considered saying that that was his temperament, but then worried the guy might think he was wising off, so he let it go. We had been in their little room a long time.

We were weary, afraid, angry. We had told them the truth: nothing was going on, nothing had happened. We didn't know the dealer, weren't sleeping with her, had no idea what they were talking about. We told them that we were good customers of the casino, that we'd played there regularly for over a year, that everyone on the graveyard shift knew us and knew how we played. We asked if they were sure they had the right guys.

They pointed to the door, told us not to come back.

Shaken and cowed, we got up and left the room, walked out and across the parking garage toward the car. We didn't look back, just got in the car and drove with ridiculous care out of the garage.

We drove to Hattiesburg in startlingly bright morning light, glad to be out of Gulfport, glad to be in the car. On the drive we rehearsed the play of the evening. What did they think was a signal? Somebody's crazy, we thought. How much did we lose? They're busting us for losing? We didn't lose enough?

13

Don't Know Quit

WHEN THE TWO security men did their little show in the windowless room, we knew trouble had arrived. These were not the happy-go-lucky types who handled the casino floor, the pits, and so forth, the people we knew. These were thugs in suits.

A few days later, Cindy, the dealer, phoned Rick. She knew that he taught at the university and called him there. She was bewildered, distraught. She had been arrested, jailed, and held overnight. The state Gaming Commission was going to hold a hearing on her license. Without the license, she couldn't work. She wanted us to testify at a commission hearing. We agreed.

After being kicked out of the casino, it didn't take us long to quit gambling; we did that instantly. For the first time in two years, the charm had gone out of it.

We were exhausted anyway, and gladly slipped back into our routine lives. Steve was teaching a Thursday night readings class, in which he was doing *The Sun Also Rises* one week, *The Master of Go* the next. He and Melanie were shopping for a car to replace the twenty-year-old Oldsmobile she had been driving, and eventually they took a loan and bought a new

Honda. For weeks they had been undecided about what color it should be. One brochure showed a deep blue car that looked charcoal in the photograph; they ordered that one. When the car arrived, they found it looked that color, but only for fifteen minutes in the early evening.

Visiting writers came and went. Thanksgiving passed. In mid-December the weather turned bitter cold, and two days before Christmas Steve and Melanie drove eleven hours to Texas, to visit her family in Austin. Rick stayed in Hattiesburg for the holidays. With Mother and Father gone, Joan and Pete having moved out of town, there was no reason to go to Houston. Rie had a birthday, early in January.

Our lives became so quotidian we could hardly believe it. We got flu shots, took walks, read, cleaned house, rented movies, went out to dinner. On Monday, January 13, the spring semester started.

During this period we didn't miss gambling. November 11 was shock therapy, showed us a side of the business that wasn't so alluring. We had an aversion to cops and jails, and these people looked like cops, only less under control. Our "addiction" suddenly looked more like a hobby, and if they wanted to hassle us, scare us, accuse us, threaten us, well, we'd get a different hobby.

Also, we felt jilted. The Grand was the best and biggest casino; it was where we wanted to go, the familiar place, the one we knew and liked, the one we felt was ours. Only it wasn't ours anymore. They were all set to arrest us if we went back.

The frenetic twenty-four- or thirty-six-hour trips, the big losses, the whole bender of the fall was over, and that was okay with us. We tried to be the exception, the ones the percentages didn't get, and we even succeeded here and there, enough to make it seem possible, but in the end we had been flattened. Like everybody else.

An advantage of being raised by our parents — our father in particular, who was a great pragmatist, and a great one for thinking himself more resourceful, more ingenious, and more resolute than any problem — was that we never felt there was anything we couldn't do. There were many things we never tried to do, many things we didn't want to do, but it never occurred to us that if we wanted to do something, we might not be able to. This kind of extraordinary haughtiness could only have been genetic, and our lives were a history of the gradual disabuse of this notion.

When we look back at our father's life and try to discover in him the schoolboy in Galveston, or the college student at Rice, or the young designer in Houston working for the society architect John Staub, or the young architect called up to Dallas to work on the Texas Centennial buildings — there to do not only the Hall of State building but also a prototype modern house, borrowed almost entirely from Le Corbusier and apparently still standing somewhere in the city — when we go over his notes from a meeting with Mies van der Rohe, during which Father apparently questioned him about his Seagram building, critical of its lack of human scale ("Mr. Barthelme, I find that I can make things beautiful, and that is enough for me," Mies had told him) — when we look back over this whole range of information, we see haughtiness, arrogance at every turn. Where did the arrogance come from?

There is a photograph of our father at the age of seven or eight. He had worn glasses from the age of three. The picture shows a dorky kid in a time when dorkiness was not as highly prized as it is today. A kid you couldn't imagine navigating the

life ahead of him successfully. It's when we look at the photograph and see our father as a child that we can guess everything that followed — all the swashbuckling, all the stories
about his conflicts with other architects, clients, university ad-
ministrators, building contractors, all the run-ins with subcon-
tractors who tried to sneak in inferior materials. Then we
imagine all of it was a reaction, a powerful and desperate reaction to the frightened condition suggested in that picture.

This wasn't something he was unaware of. Late in his life,
sitting at his desk in his upstairs office, he once said, "I knew I
was a short little guy with red hair and round glasses, and I realized real early on that if I was going to get anywhere I wasn't
going to be able to just stand there." He drew himself up and
feigned swinging his elbows. "I had to walk into a room with a
swagger, and talk loud, and tell 'em I was there."

His mother, called Mamie in our childhood, Bye to her husband and their friends, was a schoolteacher from New York
State. She drove a very strict bargain. Our mother, early in her
marriage, remembered with alarm a remark Mamie had made
about raising her children — our father and his sister, Elise: "I
always said, they may not love me, but they'll surely respect
me." Both she and Mr. Bart, our grandfather, were proud of
their boy. He apparently had plenty to work with in the brains
area. And Mamie didn't let him overlook that dimension.
But in his youth he was also well liked, one of the boys, a hell
raiser. A guy who took the risks that others wouldn't, an over-
achiever.

If he hadn't taught us to persevere, we might have given up
gambling earlier, when any sane person would have, when
it became clear we weren't going to win a fortune, when the
losses mounted. But we were people who thought we could
do anything. We were supremely gifted. If we set ourselves

the task of beating the casino, clearly it was only a matter of time before we would do just that. So what if there were a few losses in the interval between the beginning and the inevitable triumph?

The first year we had played in earnest, Rick lost fifty-four thousand dollars. Steve lost less, about thirty-nine thousand. We'd lose a few hundred or a thousand a night, and some nights two or three more. Then we'd win a thousand back, but gradually, as 1995 wore on, after our mother's death, the sums mounted. Even though we kept good records, neither of us was prepared for the amounts we totaled up at the end of the year. Rie reminded Rick about a remark he had made early in the year when he had come home after losing several thousand dollars. He had said, "Look, it's not like I'm down thirty thousand dollars or something."

Perfectly true.

Ours was an odd turn on the American myth that you can do whatever you want to do. Another aspect of the family's version of the myth led us much deeper into our losses at the casino — we rejected what everyone else believed. While everything around us told us we would lose, while all the books we read, all the people we talked to, all the information we gathered said we would lose, we just refused to believe it.

We knew better. We learned at our father's knee that any problem was solvable if you applied sufficient ingenuity and enough elbow grease. That's what we did with gambling. We worked hard to beat the casino. There's no other way to explain the marathon sessions at the blackjack tables. Every gambling book in the world cautions against such play. They say to play for an hour and take an hour break, but we knew better. Most things we'd done in life up until that time, we'd done using the same procedure — hard work, unflagging energy, singleness of purpose, an unwillingness to quit. All these good inclinations were applied to the playing of blackjack. Like our father, who had no respect for how things had been done in the past, we made up our own strategies, freely borrowing from what we read but not allowing ourselves to be limited by it.

We read books on quantum mechanics and discussed the idea that the cards weren't in any order when they were in the deck, that they came to be in an order only when they were dealt. We talked about this idea seriously. We tried to imagine how we might influence the order of the cards as they were dealt. Uri Geller, the psychic, could do it, couldn't he? Well, maybe not, but we stared at the cards and sometimes, strange as it may seem, we felt we had some communication with them. There were times when we knew what the next card was going to be, and when the card was revealed it was precisely the card we expected. This happened far too often to be thought of as coincidence, accident, chance. This was, at least, magic.

We believe to this day that many things about blackjack play and the running of the reels on slot machines and the dice at the craps table do not lend themselves readily to analysis in conventional terms; that ordinary analysis is inadequate to explain completely what cards come and when they come and why they come, what numbers show up on top of the dice, what slot the ball falls in on the roulette wheel, what happens at the baccarat table, what happens with the flip of a coin.

We believe in magic. Magic goes on. We can't explain it, can't even begin to. It's hard even to point to specific examples, but each of us has experienced it at a slot machine or a blackjack table. Each of us has been in a situation where he knew what cards were coming, knew the outcome of the game he was playing. It wasn't dependable magic, though, so its usefulness as a betting aid was limited.

One egregious example. On a certain night, Steve had won a lot of money and was waiting, killing time while Rick played blackjack, joked with the dealer, watched a nearby roulette table. We almost never played roulette. Rick picked up two green chips, handed them to Steve, pointed toward the roulette table, and looked back to the dealer, who said, "Eight."

"Fifty dollars on eight," Rick said, and Steve walked over and set the chips down on eight, a thirty-five-to-one shot, just as the dealer set the ball racing around the already spinning wheel.

"Green inside," the dealer yelled, to alert the pit boss. The pit people got nervous when anyone bet even a red chip, five dollars, on a single number, as the standard bet at roulette in these casinos was twenty-five cents or a dollar. Fifty dollars was ludicrous, unimaginable.

When the ball fell into a slot, eight was where it fell. Seventeen hundred and fifty bucks.

Magic doesn't explain how we lost a quarter million dollars over a couple of years. We lost the money because we played, because we wouldn't give up, because giving up was unheard of, because our parents were dead and there was no order to our lives. We were running free in the world, messing around, and we didn't give a shit, and nothing mattered.

We were too old to be thrilled by getting drunk or high, and dime-store sex sounded like work *and* trouble. But driving seventy miles to bet two thousand on a hand of blackjack or to put hundred-dollar bills into a slot machine, now that was a different story. That sounded like fun. We might win. Who was going to stop us? We knew it wasn't a good idea, but it didn't matter whether we did this or not. We went and lost the money. We got our credit cards jacked up to the ten-thousand-dollar limit. All it meant was that we had to pay a hundred and fifty per month in interest on each card.

Father would never approve, but Father was not watching. It was fun, weird, new. It felt like nothing we'd ever done before, and it opened up a new world of people we wouldn't otherwise have known — ordinary citizens, like people who sold clothing in department stores. Only these people weren't selling clothes; they were dealing cards or taking cards or serving drinks. Dealers, managers, players.

Most of them were busily taking our money. We didn't resent that, although we recognized it. That was their job. Dealers, for their trouble, got six dollars an hour plus tips, usually amounting to another eight or ten dollars an hour. They made good money, forty or fifty thousand a year, more than they would have made anywhere else. They seemed pleased to be dealing, but conflicted about taking our money. Ditto the pit bosses and the casino hosts. They were concerned, suggested we leave when our losses mounted, were pleased to send us back to Hattiesburg in limousines when that seemed warranted, or to put us up in hotels, or to comp us two-hundred-dollar meals at their steak restaurant, where the filet went for thirty-eight dollars and the potato for twelve.

We went and we played and we lost. We had hope, but the hope was groundless and we lost. We had plans, strategies, though not very well constructed nor very well carried out and we lost. The only thing we did that would have made our father proud was that we did not give up, we never threw up our hands and said we can't do this. We never really quit.

In hindsight, of course, we wish this was a lesson we had learned rather less well. We would be better off.

From the casino's vantage, they lost money by expelling us. Maybe they didn't stop to think, Wait a minute, these two mooks are just giving us money. Instead they kicked us out, accused us of all kinds of grotesque business, and cut themselves out of a hundred thousand dollars, which we managed to lose in the course of 1997 at another casino, where we played the same games for the same reasons in the same ways and with the same results.

If Father hadn't taught us a tenacity that boggles the mind, if he hadn't shown us what it's like to believe yourself to the exclusion of all other evidence, if we hadn't replicated his own anarchic arrogance, if he hadn't taught us always to imagine the self as better than the other, then surely the moment would have come in this bottle-rocket gambling trajectory when recognition would have set in and we would have slowed the pace, shrugged, and said, well, there's one thing we can't do. But that didn't happen.

14

Next Year

FOR PEOPLE raised Catholic, trained to ferret out the sin hidden in every hiccup, just being accused of cheating was unsettling. Suddenly, in imagination, the casino had all this *authority*. Who would have predicted that? We'd never thought of the casino as having any authority before. It wasn't an institution like, say, the highway patrol or the Church. It was Wal-Mart with a high flashing-light content. But now all the lines connecting the casino to the police, to the sovereign state of Mississippi, to the "justice system," to the Gaming Commission — all entities whose gaze you did not seek — were drawn taut. We'd always avoided attracting attention, paid our bills on time, filed the proper forms, stopped on red and gone on green; now we understood why.

In the weeks after the November 11 incident, we taught our classes, watched television, raked the yard, went to the supermarket as usual, but we were rattled. Being treated like criminals is a bewildering, stunning disenfranchisement, and even though at that point we weren't crossed up with the law, the fact that the casino had surrounded us, intimidated us, interrogated us, ordered us out, and threatened us with arrest was sufficient. We *felt* like criminals. For middle-class boys, that was scary. We poked and prodded our memories of the night, going round and round about what had happened. Were they after the dealer or us? Why would they be after us?

When you're treated badly by a large organization, it makes you angry, but it also makes you think how powerful the organization is, how much it contributes to the local economy, to the political infrastructure, to political parties, to campaigns, candidates, judges. Casinos in Mississippi contribute a lot. So now, as you're reading a magazine, you notice that the leading contributors to political campaigns are the insurance companies, tobacco companies, and "gaming interests." This makes you realize how little you count in the grand scheme of things.

Shortly after our ouster, Rick wrote a gentle, naïve letter to the head of gaming at the Grand Casino, declaring our innocence and saying we hoped it would all get straightened out.

No reply. We didn't hear a word from the casino or from the dealers, pit people, floor managers, casino hosts — all the folks who worked the swing and graveyard shifts and with whom we'd had plenty of contact — people we imagined might speak up and explain everything to the casino's management. We were certain the corporate types would catch this mistake before it got out of hand, that someone would look into it and then the ban would be rescinded, the incident recatalogued as a misunderstanding.

Did not happen.

Around this time Cindy, the dealer, called Rick at the university, as mentioned before, to report what had happened to her and to see what had happened to us. She offered no explanation. She'd been arrested and charged, her dealer's license revoked, and she wanted to know if we'd been charged too. As far as we knew, we hadn't. Cindy had been taken to the Harrison County Jail, held for hours until she could post bond. She couldn't get her license back without a hearing before the Gaming Commission, a creature of the casinos, so she was out of work and would be unable to work in another casino until she was cleared. The Grand and the Gaming Commission were bearing down on her.

We felt bad for her but were glad we hadn't been arrested. Then we felt bad for feeling that. We found out a year later that warrants had been issued for our arrest, but they had been put on hold by the district attorney pending further investigation. Still, any cop or trooper who stopped one of us for speeding and happened to check the NCIC — the National Crime Information Center, a law enforcement database — would have found that we were wanted and given us a fast trip to jail in the back of a police car. Happily, we didn't know that then, so we went on our way right through Christmas and New Year's, chastened and disinclined to go to the casino. Forbidden, in fact, to go to the Grand. The whole gambling parade had turned poisonous.

At the beginning of 1997, we had been asked to testify for Cindy before the Gaming Commission hearing. We agreed to do so, but the lesson of thirty years of TV cop shows was: get a lawyer. So we asked several lawyers in Hattiesburg and they recommended Boyce Holleman, a former D.A. in Gulfport, now a defense attorney.

On January 31 we sat in squeaky leather chairs in the cramped waiting area of the Holleman law office, watching a big yellow fish swim around in an aquarium. It was the only fish in the water. A photograph on the wall showed a youngish man, presumably Boyce Holleman, with three boys and a girl, the children proudly lined up in front of him. It was apparently an old picture; we noticed a few Hollemans were stenciled on the glass door of the place, in the law practice with him.

We were called back to the big office at the end of the hall. Holleman was polite and friendly, in his seventies, and he listened to our story with his eyes closed most of the time, occasionally lurching forward to drink root beer from a glass bottle. When the bottle was empty, he tossed it over his shoulder into the wastebasket. He was a character. A most complicated character, as you never had the slightest doubt — he well knew the dramatic effect of every grimace, gesture, and offhand remark.

He had bushy but thinning hair, the ugliest unlit cigar you ever saw, cowboy boots, a cane, and a drawl worthy of the movies (we learned later that he had used it, playing small roles in the television series *In the Heat of the Night* and in several movies shot in the area). The office, a down-at-the-heels wood-paneled ranch-style house about three blocks off the water, was peppered with Holleman's memorabilia — photos of him chatting with Bob Hope, standing in front of an airplane with his crew as a World War II pilot, with Carroll O'Connor. There was a framed note from JFK.

We'd been told that Boyce Holleman was the best defense lawyer in the region, and meeting him produced in us an odd joy such as you might feel upon finally meeting the Wizard in Oz. Because of the wonderful things he does. On our way home that day, we felt that having him on our side, notwithstanding that he had seemed almost asleep for much of our conference, was powerfully reassuring. From then on, we always called him *Mr.* Holleman, out of a special respect.

He told us he played some blackjack himself, and he was no fan of the gaming laws. Under Mississippi law, he said, all gaming violations were felonies. Some kid takes a dollar token out of a slot tray, its a goddam felony, he snorted.

He told us a story he'd heard about an old man who sat down on a slot machine stool to rest when some casino people came over with all this money, a payoff for somebody else's jackpot. "You know, he hadn't looked where he was, he's just sitting there. He's takin' a load off. These people were giving him money, and so he said sure." Mr. Holleman held his hand out, accepting the imaginary money, and shrugged. "They arrested him, charged him with a felony."

We told him about the dealer's Gaming Commission hearing, which was scheduled for early February, that we had agreed to testify in Cindy's behalf, and that we were to be subpoenaed in any case. He said he didn't think the hearing was a good idea for the dealer. The Gaming Commission likely favored the casinos, and their decision might influence any legal case, in spite of the hearings not being a proper legal proceeding. On the other hand, he said, if a legal case went first, its good outcome would make the commission's case easier for the dealer.

When the subpoenas arrived in the mail, we sent them to Mr. Holleman, and he called Cindy's lawyer, Frank Wittman, and said we weren't going to testify, explained why, and the two lawyers agreed that the dealer should postpone her Gaming Commission hearing indefinitely, to await what we all hoped would be the dropped charges in her criminal case. At worst, a trial and an acquittal.

We were happy to dodge the invitation to testify, but we felt bad for Cindy, who was in limbo and without a license to work. She was getting a raw deal from the D.A. and the Gaming Commission, which had taken away her livelihood. It seemed that they were covering their backsides for having done this in the first place. The casino had plenty to lose if the dealer could prove her prosecution was "malicious."

In the months after March 1997, when the commission hearing was put on hold, nothing happened in the case. The dealer had been charged, but no further move had been made against her; as far as we knew, we were not being charged. We allowed ourselves to believe that Mr. Holleman's easygoing attitude had been right all along, that we'd been a touch hysterical. We allowed ourselves to believe that the whole regrettable mess had faded away. We hoped that, anyway.

Sometime in May, as the fear that had gripped us abated, we started going back to the casinos. Steve first, Rick later. We settled on Biloxi's Casino Magic, an architectural curiosity, faux modern, replete with violently exposed steelwork, strange angles, severe shapes. Inside, it was just a barge, a big hall open from one end to the other. It was smaller than the Grand, but the people were pleasant and we began making friends and losing money there. At the Magic we became known as "the brothers." When one of us would go alone, they would ask where the other was. Occasionally we ran into dealers from the Grand — some of them were now working at the Magic — and so we wondered whether the news of our difficulties with the Grand had spread. When a security man stood nearby and watched a game, as they often did, we became anxious. We were gun-shy, edgy. But after a while the Magic grew comfortable and inviting. The personnel weren't as eager to glad-hand the players — slap you on the back, smile wide, talk family — and they weren't nearly as deferential, but that was fine with us. Later in the year, we found out that they had known about the trouble at the Grand all along. For them, being eighty-sixed at the Grand didn't mean we were guilty of anything, and that bit of fairness and good sense made us very fond of the Magic.

It became our regular shop in summer 1997. We went once a

week, sometimes twice. We had what seemed markedly better luck there than we had had at the Grand, so much better that it was striking, and set us to wondering.

Gradually our gambling got furious again. We went more often, stayed longer hours, played harder, lost more money. In the late summer and fall we made about thirty trips to the Magic. In one night's play, Rick lost twenty-three thousand dollars. Altogether, we lost eighty thousand dollars.

Gambling had never made sense to us, but its incoherence was not troubling; its illogic was part of its charm. We realized how little we remembered about all the gambling we'd done over the past last few years. We kept meticulous records as far as the money went — how much we lost, how much we won back, when we did, when we didn't. And both of us remembered the *feeling* of gambling, the moment the air conditioning hit us, the sounds — jingling, chatter, shouting. Dealers in their costumes, red vests, bow ties, string ties, tux shirts. The rush of things picking up speed, beginning to hurtle.

One night during this time, to treat a visiting writer, we brought her to Casino Magic. We bet for her — five hundred dollars a hand, a thousand dollars a hand. We had started playing around midnight, won and lost, and finally, in the wee hours of the morning, Rick came into a couple of big hands of blackjack, broke even or better, and cashed in. Then he left, with Steve still deep in the hole, bound to play all the next day and into the next night until he too could break even, get ahead a few hundred dollars, then leave.

We had taken this visitor, the poet Lucie Brock-Broido, thinking she might be a little charmed, and that we would mess around a bit, show her the coast, the casinos, the slots, and so on. But that hadn't happened. The minute we got into the casino, we sat down in the high-stakes blackjack area and started playing seriously, and we didn't let up until many hours later. In other words, it was like always: arrive around midnight, lose a bundle at first, spend the rest of the night trying to get it back, leave the next day. It's typical. Within minutes we're over our heads, bets ratcheting up fast until they're so big they're silly. We try to limit the carnage, but still, things happen. Like a night in January 1998, well after we've been indicted, Rick loses $22,000 in six hours. It takes all of 1998 to reduce that to a bearable $6,000 loss for the year. Steve wins $132,000 at the slots in 1997. He loses $150,000. We compare notes about specific machines, think we've got them diced out, then we start talking to the reels as they whirl around. We get so we can see a hit coming — register the stop of the first reel and refocus on the second before it starts to slow. We read more about quantum mechanics, imagine how it applies to slots, to cards. Meanwhile, the casino treats us well. People jump at the slightest signal from us, the wonder of our Hansel-and-Gretel trail of cash. And when we leave for the coast we know the outcome. Ten minutes out of Hattiesburg, on the Heart of Darkness Turnpike headed for Gulfport, when one says "I'm going to lose thousands tonight, Jesus," the other says, invariably, "You want to turn around?" There's a pause, laughter, and we drive on with grim determination, gallows humor, excitement. We have made peace with the last loss and are ready to go again. So each night begins. One of us picks up the other and we drive into the Mississippi darkness, headed for a place where everything is different.

All through the summer and fall of 1997, we had heard nothing and figured the Grand fiasco was over. Then, in December, about thirteen months after the incident, Cindy called our office once again. She had been indicted by a grand jury, she told Rick, and we were named in the indictment. Cindy wasn't sure whether we had also been indicted, just that we were named. We didn't quite know what that meant, but assumed the worst.

Rick then told Rie, who went to tell Steve, who was upstairs teaching a class, an undergraduate story workshop. Steve stepped outside the classroom into the hall, afraid that Rick had become ill, since it was extremely unusual for Rie, who worked at *Mississippi Review,* to interrupt a class.

"Cindy from the coast called," she said. "You've been indicted." Steve asked her to repeat it, and she did. He nodded, a sick feeling settling in his stomach. "I'll be back down in the office after this class," he said.

What we eventually discovered was that in September 1997, ten months after the original incident, an indictment was issued and we were formally charged with the crime of conspiring to cheat the casino by "acquiring knowledge, not available to all players," from the dealer. All three of us were listed on the same indictment. In the period from January to December 1997, we were never told that we had been or were to be charged, nor were our lawyers. In fact, our lawyers weren't even told that the indictment had been issued in September. They heard it from us on the day Cindy called.

That the D.A. had obtained arrest warrants almost a year before and then decided not to execute them until "further investigation" seemed a peculiar bit of legal maneuvering. In "discovery" materials supplied later, nothing suggested any further investigation had been done. Mr. Holleman told us the D.A. probably wanted a grand jury indictment, but why he had waited nine months we did not know.

It seemed impossibly baroque, after a year of silence, to suddenly find out that we had been indicted. We contacted Mr. Holleman immediately and told him what Cindy had told us. He got together with her lawyer, then talked to the county sheriff and arranged for us to be booked and released on our own recognizance. A week later, on a chill December morning, we drove down to Gulfport and searched out the Harrison County Jail.

15

Booked

WHAT YOU MOST want to know when being arrested for the first time is, How long is this going to take? Or, more properly, How long will this last? It bears a resemblance to surgery, full of familiar terms whose full meanings just aren't in the brain. You want to know, Will there be handcuffs? Will I be put in a cell? Who else is likely to be in the cell? When the lawyer's assistant says you'll be quickly booked and released, does she know what she's talking about?

Friday, December 12, 1997, was rainy and cold, one of the gray days of winter that seem to stretch endlessly from November through March. We drove down to Gulfport to turn ourselves in to police at the Harrison County Jail, to be booked, fingerprinted, and processed on a charge of felony conspiracy in a supposed plan to bilk the Grand Casino.

Our surrender had been arranged by Mr. Holleman, who by this time we had learned was a legend of Gulf Coast lawyering — twenty years a D.A., once president of the Mississippi Bar Association, a former state legislator, a movie actor, a man who had "Boulevard" after his name, as in Boyce Holleman Boulevard in Gulfport, the street on which the county courthouse sat in the little city where we were charged. At the jail, Mr. Holleman was well known. Someone asked if we'd been sent by the father or one of the sons. The father, they were told. The fact that the jail people were careful about the Hollemans impressed us a great deal.

We would turn ourselves in and be booked "in and out," a phrase that we held dear, implying as it did a perfunctory procedure. Mr. Holleman had been at the jail the week before for a meeting of a prison building committee, on which he sat, and he took that opportunity to chat with the sheriff, explain our situation — two college professors indicted for cheating the casino — and arrange for this surrender. Neither of us had ever seen the inside of a jail, except for the usual high school drinking and drag-racing incidents. What we knew of prison we knew mainly from gaudy and dramatic movies and from Frederick Wiseman–style documentaries. While we numbered some criminals among our acquaintances, jails were pretty much virgin territory for us.

The overcast was daunting and the light rain was turning to sleet. We drove around the industrial wasteland north of Gulfport, between the city and the major east-west artery of I-10, six lanes of high-speed traffic shooting from Florida to West Texas and beyond. There was a not-tiny airport tucked back in the marshy weeds, trees clustered in tight stands, too many metal buildings to count, and a few huge industrial plants, all silver spires and ladders and Erector-set loveliness. In ordinary circumstances, we might have admired the architecture of those plants, triumphs of industrial realism, but that day we just wove around on the bare concrete and the unfinished lanes that cut through the weeds, dodging trucks piled high with refinery equipment and watching the white dust jumping up off the road with every passing car, until we found the Harrison

County Jail, three stories of generic yellow brickwork decorated with uncommonly shiny razor wire. We rolled in past the threatening signs and parked in the blacktop lot behind the place, one of a handful of civilian cars among two dozen cop cruisers, with whip antennas and big badge decals on their doors. A long concrete walk sloped up to the entrance of the jail. We got out of the car and stood for a moment in the damp air, dressed up in jeans, nice button-down shirts, suit coats — college professors.

What we saw inside was a large X-shaped room, some muscle-bound gray steel doors off to the right, with metal detectors circling them and lights above them, some plastic benches screwed into walls as in a bus station. Forlorn-looking people sat around in groups: two children, a mother, and an older woman; a girl with a clingy shirt and lots of black hair sitting with two teenage boys, one holding a baby of maybe six months; three generations of women — a daughter, a mother, a grandmother; and various police officers, many of whom were short and all of whom seemed to like their uniforms tight. That's *tight*. The big glass panel that sat diagonally in front of us as we walked in was dark, like limo glass, and it didn't seem to have an opening.

A woman was talking to the glass, and people were stacked up in a line behind her. So we got in the line, and as our eyes became acclimated, we made out two policemen sitting behind the tint. We asked to be directed to the deputy sheriff's office. We'd been given his name by Mr. Holleman's assistant.

The deputy sheriff came out to greet us. He shook our hands, invited us to follow him out of this public lobby, through a regular door off to the left, to a secretary's desk, where he explained to the woman who we were and why we were there.

He seemed confused about how to act. One minute he was polite and the next a little brusque, as if he couldn't figure out which he was supposed to be. He told us to stand there while the secretary fetched a detective who was going to do the "jackets" on us. It was all very civilized, like renewing your driver's license. This wasn't so bad.

The plainclothes detective took Rick back to sit beside a desk in a small, three-walled cubicle, a space maybe seven feet square. The guy had a big wad of tobacco in his cheek, but he was calm and pleasant. He took down information, asked questions — date of birth, place of employment, ever been arrested before — and every now and again he leaned to the side and spat consummately into the trash can alongside his desk.

Steve was next. He walked back past three or four cubicles with empty desks, to the plainclothesman's "office." The guy was well dressed, informal, and looked like someone standing on his lawn on a Sunday afternoon. He was still working on his chewing tobacco and said he'd been bothered by the flu for God knows how long. "But I can't stand staying home with her," he said. "She'll drive me crazy. Worse than working." It was creepy — the detective was way too friendly.

Meanwhile, the cop who had brought us in from outside, the deputy sheriff, told Rick to take a seat in a waiting room, a little jag in the corridor where there were a couple of chairs and some fingerprinting equipment. After a minute, Rick got up and went hunting for a bathroom. The cops pointed him toward a men's room, but once he was inside somebody banged loudly on the door, and there was a round of big laughter outside. Rick opened the door. The new cop standing there instantly stopped laughing and raised an eyebrow. "Oh, sorry. I thought you were somebody else," he said.

Rie, who had come along with us, was waiting in the X-shaped lobby. Before entering the jail, Steve had taken off his watch and handed it to her — he didn't want to sit in a cell with a watch on; it seemed wrong somehow, and he also didn't want to lose it; it had been a gift from a favorite student ten years before. Rie wasn't allowed in the business end of the jail; the back was only for criminals and cops. The office section, where the two of us sat with the spitting detective, had corkboards lining the walls, like a fifties grade school, and was painted in that two-tone way schools were always painted, as if the wainscoting were brushed on. The other decorations and appointments — things tacked to the walls, or taped there, and the desks and dividers — also looked as if they belonged in a grammar school.

When Steve got back, accompanied by the detective, the three of us went to a place in the corridor where there was more fingerprinting gear. The guy did our prints, one at a time, rolling each finger carefully on the inkpad and then carefully on the form, making the prints almost square. Then he did them again, in weird groupings — four fingers together and no thumb, odd pairs, and so on. When the form was filled, the detective gave us restroom paper towels and some grease-cutting solvent in a plastic spray bottle and we cleaned up as he walked us down a hallway, past an elevator, around a corner, and into the mug-shot room. He told Steve to stand in the corridor while he took Rick in for pictures. Steve went looking for the men's room, which was by the elevator.

The mug-shot room was like a soft-drink and snacks room at a Holiday Inn — tiny, close. There was a candy machine in the room, loaded with Butterfinger bars. Lots of other clutter. The face of an old refrigerator with rounded edges bore a taped-on handwritten sign that read, RAPE KITS. DO NOT OPEN. A Polaroid camera was mounted on an elaborate metal apparatus, like a piece of exercise equipment, a standard distance from the subject. The detective told Rick to stand in front of the backdrop, which was marked in feet and inches right up to eight feet and change, making you wonder how many eight-foot-tall men they got in the jail. "Look at the camera, look away, then look back at the camera," the detective said in a monotone, something he'd probably said a thousand times. He snapped a couple of shots.

This was still the same friendly Sunday afternoon cop, in his khakis and plaid short-sleeved shirt. He finished with Rick and went out to get Steve, only Steve couldn't be found. The detective jerked up and down the corridor, went back out by the elevator, yelled. All of a sudden there was this adrenaline in the air.

Steve heard the sharp, urgent shouts. He walked out of the men's room and stopped, looking both ways. It didn't occur to him that the disturbance was about him until he saw the detective's stiff face. "I'm sorry," Steve said, and gestured to the men's room door. "Don't do that," the detective said.

Standing in the corridor, Rick thought, Why don't we just get out of here? But then he remembered that it was jail and he and Steve were the prisoners. At this point the real meaning of prison started to edge into consciousness.

An attractive young woman in an office down the hall from the snack and mug-shot room was unpacking a cardboard carton. She had a small yellow boom box playing rock 'n' roll music, something ironically familiar, that faux-naïve voice singing, "What if God were one of us . . ."

Finally the detective finished taking Steve's pictures, and the three of us were standing in the corridor again. For a moment we were thinking, Was that it? This really had not been so bad, maybe some more paperwork, sign something or other? We'd had files made, each had been given a copy of a form that said something along these lines: "TO THE SHERIFF OF HARRISON COUNTY / GREETINGS. We command you to take Steven Barthelme wheresoever he may be found in your County, and him safely keep, so that you have his body before the Circuit Court of Harrison County, Mississippi INSTANTER, then and there to answer . . . ," etc., etc. We had been ordered around, fingerprinted and photographed, and spoken to in serious tones of voice — now we could go home. We felt better, but a little drained. Mr. Holleman's assistant was right, we thought; it had taken just twenty minutes.

But then the spitting detective said, "This way," and led us down the hall to the elevator. We got on and dropped to the basement. The cops there wore uniforms and worked in a room behind a counter on one side of a wide concrete corridor. Opposite them, across the corridor, were sealed, glass-faced cinderblock holding cells with stainless steel cots along one side and low, three-foot-square cinderblock screens coming out from the opposite walls, hiding toilets. Turned out this was where we were actually going to be booked. What had gone on up until then, the civilized business with the detective, wasn't really booking. Booking was down here, in the gut of the building.

The walls were painted this soothing gray-green, and the Cyclone fencing above the counter separating the cops from the rest of us was a restful gray. The room crawled with cops, popping out of their uniforms, buttons bursting, seams swollen. Our side of the wire was full of men in oversize short-sleeved orange coveralls, black kids mostly. Behind us were the glassed-in cells and in front of us a kind of kennel for cops, behind the heavy chain-link fence that ran from countertop to ceiling. One guy stood behind the counter and was handling the business, with others standing beside him or milling around behind him. People were buzzed in or out of the kennel. Half a dozen brown paper grocery bags with black Magic Marker writing on them sat on a table against the back wall. The detective who had brought us told us to stand at the counter. The guy behind the counter said something, and the detective turned to us and said, "You-all aren't carrying guns, are you?" and laughed. He was buzzed into the cage and talked to the other guy, a short muscular policeman, not more than five foot five but very puffed in his uniform. Our guy told the short guy that Mr. Holleman wanted us booked in and booked out, and it was clear that this was an instruction: do it now, don't wait.

"*Mr.* Holleman?" the short cop said, checking to be sure.

"Right. In and out," the detective said. "They go O.R."

The short cop talked to a bristly blond cop next to him, who was considerably larger and constantly yelling at the people waiting out in the corridor. "Get back there, nigger," the blond cop shouted. "Don't do that to me. Pull up those pants," he said, making some kind of finger-pointing gesture. "And don't put your hands on my window, either. Stand back. Quit bending around like that."

Things were okay as long as the upstairs detective was handling us, but after he had given our files to the short cop in uniform, pointed us out, and told the guy what Mr. Holleman wanted, he left. So we were stuck there with this small, powerful cop with short dark hair and a bigger, heavier blond guy whose stock-in-trade seemed to be ragging inmates. This was too much like TV to be comfortable, and it wasn't clear which was chicken and which egg — reality begetting TV or the other

way around. The two of us stood eyeing each other and the activity around us, not moving much.

There was lots of testosterone running loose down there in
the basement. The blond cop and a couple of others who came
and went were yelling at the kids — almost everybody down
there was a kid, seventeen to twenty — and the kids were
toughing it out, doing that hitched, rolling walk, wearing the
dangerously lowball pants, and playing street tough. It was all
about aggression, muscle, power, turf, bob-and-weave. That
and grocery-bag luggage.

Then began a series of distractions. A guy getting released
came out from where the main jail was, down to our left,
and he had to be processed. He got his paper sack of street
clothes and changed into them. The blond cop said, "Pull up
those pants, Bama," and when the guy didn't, he told him
again. "I just might lose your paperwork, you be in here
Christmas."

We were told to step back and stand in front of the windows
of the holding cells with some other people being processed,
and we did, both of us standing rail-straight in our suit coats.
Next to Steve, a black woman in the standard orange coveralls
did a little inspection and then said, "You important? You look
important." Steve shook his head. "What are you guys? CIA?"
she said. "Are you guys CIA?" Steve shook his head again,
then nodded toward Rick and said, "He's CIA." We didn't
laugh, just sort of smiled, keeping our eyes forward, but then
killed the smile entirely, not knowing what it might look like.
Smiling wasn't real big down here, and a smirk seemed like a
bad idea. No facial expression whatsoever would be about perfect. We were thinking military bearing, what we wanted was
military bearing.

"You're plainclothes," the woman said, satisfying herself. "You got a cigarette?"

We both said no. We didn't actually say it, just shook our heads. We wanted to laugh with her, make jokes, but we were too careful for that. A cop came up to her at that point and put handcuffs on her, and when she asked him for a cigarette, he gave her a quick lecture about smoking "up there" and how she knew it would just get her into trouble. They were apparently long-time acquaintances.

She had leg cuffs on, and he led her over to a group of orange-coveralled kids gathered around the exit, seven black guys lined up waiting to get on a bus we could see parked in the sloped loading dock outside. Another cop pushed these guys against the wall, one after another. He told them to back up, and if they didn't he gave them a little shove. The guys were all wearing handcuffs, which looked flimsy, like Dick Tracy handcuffs you might buy at a toy store. They were serious handcuffs but they looked damn thin, as if the manufacturer had figured a way to make an extra dollar on every pair by squinching on the materials. There was a shiny pile of them on the end of the counter where all the business was being transacted. Now we were the only people left standing in the lineup in front of the holding cells.

A cop brought in a white man who looked like somebody out of a Tennessee Williams play — thin, pale, wearing brown pleated slacks, a white linen shirt, a skinny tie. The short cop circled out from behind the cage, pulling on a pair of slick black gloves. He told the guy to lean forward and grab the counter, and then he patted him down, careful to check the waistband of his slacks. He took the guy's tie, belt, shoes, and the stuff from his pockets and put it all in a brown paper bag and wrote on it. Somebody brought the guy a pair of the orange plastic sandals all the prisoners wore, and two cops walked him over to the last holding cell, which had only a small window in the door. The other holding cells had one or two occupants, but when the door to this one opened, it looked like a dozen people were in there. All kids, pretty much all black.

Now two new cops brought two new black guys in. The cops were thin and smaller than their prisoners. The new cops wanted these guys booked right away. The short cop behind the counter tried to explain that he had us to deal with, but the two cops with the fresh captures said fuck that, do their guys first. Our cop turned to the big blond cop and asked him, and there was some discussion after which the blond cop stared hard at us for a minute and said something like, "Fuck upstairs. I don't care what they want done. Do the new ones first." So the short cop started on that, and then the blond cop had another idea and said, "Just get them in Holding One and then go on and finish the other two."

One of the cops who had brought in the two black guys got into a shoving match with their charges. It was as if the cops wanted to have this fight, it was like a diagram of a fight. The black guy said, "Get out of my face." The cop squared off and said, "I'm in your face. What are you gonna do about it?"

The black kid muttered something about "Not here," and the cop snorted. "What do you mean? Everybody here," he said, looking around at us, "is on your side."

Got that right, we thought.

There were lots of under-the-breath *shit*s and *fuck*s, but the black guy wasn't going to do anything, apparently. His friend and the other cop were just standing around waiting. The little cop behind the counter said, "How many pairs of pants he wearing there?"

One of the new cops said, "How many pairs of pants you wearing?"

"I don't know, man," the kid said.

Together the cops decided the kid was wearing too many pairs of pants, so they told him to take off all the pants except one pair. Turned out he was wearing four pairs of pants, each waistband peeking up under the next. To get out of the pants, he had to drop his sneaks. The short cop came out from behind the cage, pulling on his black gloves to pat down the kid and his friend.

The blond cop said, "What size shoe you wear?"

"Eleven," the kid said.

The cop hollered, "Gimme a twelve!" to some trusty down at the other end of the hall. The trusty, a white kid, looked like a girl — close-cropped hair, all bent-back elbows and willow walk as he ducked into a room to our right and came out with a pair of the Day-Glo orange flipflops, the number 13 clearly marked in the heel. One of the cops gave the black kid a fresh grocery bag and told him to put his shoes and the extra pants in it.

Instead, he started taking off his shirts. He had two or three on, but went all the way down to bare skin in a last effort at defiance. He was going to outdo the cop.

It didn't happen. Cop said, "You can go in with your cock hanging loose, I don't care." The kid shrugged his bare shoulders. The short cop patted the two of them down, again carefully checking the waistbands of their pants, and they were walked over and put in the overcrowded holding cell.

We were still in front of the window of one of the holding cells, where we'd been standing for better than half an hour. Each cubicle had a different specimen in it. One, just behind us to the right, held two or three scraggly fifty-year-old white women weighing sixty or seventy pounds apiece. One kept trying to take off her clothes, and the guys moving through the corridor stopped to look at her, making jokes, laughing. The blond hands-on cop kept yelling at her to put her clothes back on, threatening to go in there and put them on her himself.

Behind us, in the next cell, there was a sick-looking white kid wrapped in a blanket. He was on the stainless steel cot, but every once in a while he got up and wandered in the cell, the blanket around him Indian style. He tapped on the glass, asked us for a cigarette, making cigarette-lighting motions with his hands. He was yelling, we could barely hear him, but somehow the tough-guy blond cop, who was twenty feet away across the corridor, heard him perfectly.

He yelled for the kid to shut up, then reached down and pulled a cigarette out of a pack, some unfiltered brand, Lucky Strike maybe, lit up and took a deep drag, blew the smoke out slowly, trying a couple of rings. "No smokin' down here, boy!" he shouted. "That's against the goddam rules."

Meanwhile, the short cop, the one who was doing the actual booking, decided to work on our jackets. He went through the whole process again — took down some information, walked each of us over to a corner, got us to stand in front of a giant ruler, took our photographs with a camera hooked to a computer. He was behind a side window working the computer while we stood out in the open. When he was done, he told us to stand in front of the cells again.

Things were taking a long time, longer than we figured. We'd seen the sights and were ready to move on, but we couldn't change the channel, couldn't do anything but wait for this short cop with the bushy black hair to tell us what next. But that was better than the alternative, the hardass blond cop in charge. Guys who were in for drugs and robbery acted as if they lived this all the time; they were used to it, used to pushing at cops, used to fighting back within the boundaries of what the cops allowed. That was probably better than feeling powerless, but we didn't have a clue about how to play the game, and we weren't there to risk anything. Plus, we were lucky: we would get to leave in about an hour. Everyone else, on both sides of the wire, was in it for the long term. For them, every day was constant threat and counterthreat. They could get clipped any minute.

This was cop country, and you didn't want to cross them. But that was tricky, because if you were too polite they might figure you were a smartass. Still, there wasn't any percentage in arguing. The real cops and the real criminals made this world genuinely scary. It was a place of TV clichés — nice cop, loudmouth cop, mean cop, swishy inmate, crazy inmate, cut-you inmate — except these folks were serious; they didn't think they were a show. One stupid move and you were the motherfucker the cop was yelling at, and you got the sense he could do some damage if he had to.

So we were thankful we had Mr. Holleman's name on our paperwork, because nobody seemed to want to mess with Mr. Holleman. And even at that, we couldn't be sure. Who was to say these particular cops were going to stay in line? The whole operation looked pretty short-fused. If something slipped we could be down there a month. We might capture the imagination of one of the resident sadists, who weren't in short supply. We weren't naïve enough to believe the system was going to protect us. The system had put us there.

*

We saw the world outside the jail through the eyes of our father, whose dearest wish was that the world would make sense, that virtue would be rewarded and idiocy cast out.

Our father wasn't inclined to ignore what he actually saw, which was an entirely capricious world. One Sunday afternoon in the fifties he picked up a phonograph record and read the label. "Unbreakable?" he said, and he bent it and bent it until the record finally snapped. "Not unbreakable," he said, and shook his head. That was his style, and it became part of ours, a part that sometimes caused problems because the skepticism made it hard to talk to people who believed stuff. They were on some other wavelength, from some other side of town.

But at the Harrison County Jail we were like the bewildered character in the commercial who does the twist in a vain attempt to get his "Twist to Open" cap unscrewed. We didn't live there, we didn't know how we got there, we didn't know how it worked. If the world outside look capricious, the world in the basement was mad.

Eventually the booking was done. The cops finished with us and then, suddenly, in that instant hindsight, it hadn't seemed so terrible. It had taken about two hours. When the last paper was signed, the second sets of inky fingers wiped semi-clean with spray bottle and brown toilet towels, out came the stocky, muscular cop from behind his fence. He walked us to a door at the far end of the corridor. He was solicitous. He asked if we were all right, if we'd gotten our hands clean. He showed us to a stairwell and said, "Just right up here — that'll take you to the main waiting area." We thanked him and smiled and went through the door he opened for us, into the stairwell. Six or seven guys in orange overalls came down the stairs, followed by two in uniform. The overalled guys stood aside and the cops let us pass, staring at us quizzically, not sure what to make of us in our suit coats.

Upstairs, we found Rie in the entrance area and hustled out of the building. It was very still outside. Cold, raining, sleety, just as gray as two hours before. Rie handed over Steve's watch and did not ask how things had gone.

As we crossed the parking lot, we laughed nervously and beamed amazement and relief. We looked over our shoulders, as if they might come retrieve us. One of us joked that spending the next two years there would be good for our careers, lending authenticity. And then we were in the car, winding our way out of the industrial park and up to the interstate, then on the highway aiming for the turnoff that would take us back to Hattiesburg and our ordinary lives.

We stopped at a gas station to fill up the car. Rick went inside and bought a Butterfinger.

Back on the highway, we could see the jail through a break in the carefully planned row of obscuring trees, and it looked harmless, benign, and most of all foreign, a place we didn't belong. That Talking Heads song "Once in a Lifetime" came on the radio, on an oldies station. The mock-astonished voice of David Byrne washed us with its made-to-order irony. How did we get here? Our story, like a lot of others, fit the song perfectly, but it didn't seem so funny, and it wouldn't soon be over.

16

Insurance

IN BLACKJACK, taking insurance is a defensive play that
can be used when the dealer gets an ace up. The dealer is
supposed to look at her hole card and find out if she has a
blackjack, but not until she asks the players if they want insurance. She doesn't actually pick up the hole card, but instead
checks it by slipping the cards into a mirror device built into
the table in front of her, a "peeker."

Blackjack play often goes very fast, as many as a hundred
hands an hour dealt. The casino's manual for dealers pre-
scribes a method for offering and "closing" the insurance part
of the game: a sweep of the hand from one end of the table to
the other to open insurance betting, a pause while players take
or don't take insurance, and then an announcement that insurance is closed, often with a second wave of the hand. After
these gestures, the insurance betting is finished, and the dealer
is allowed to look at her hole card.

In practice, this elaborate procedure is rarely followed. Sea-
soned dealers develop their own abbreviated versions of the
routine, and especially when playing with regular customers,
or in the blackjack salon, the open and close can be reduced to

a nod or a glance. Most of the dealers who follow the full procedure are brand-new ones. Often the invitation for insurance is done orally instead of by hand signal. At a hundred hands an hour, insurance is taken or not taken very quickly, and it's not unusual to be sitting at a table with a fast dealer who closes insurance before you've decided whether or not to take it. Unless you're willing to make a scene, you're usually out of luck.

The insurance bet is half your original bet on the hand. If you take insurance and the dealer has blackjack, the hand is over but you don't lose anything — you have "insured," or protected, your money. But if she doesn't have blackjack, you instantly lose the insurance bet and then the rest of the hand is played out as usual, and you either win or lose your original bet based on the cards that are dealt.

Insurance is really a way to get you to make what is, oddswise, a bad bet. "It's a twenty-eight-percent bet!" Mr. Holleman was fond of exclaiming — meaning you lose it seventy-two percent of the time. The blackjack books tend to agree with him: it's a lousy bet. Professional blackjack players almost never take it. It's only good when the deck is ten-rich, which means the deck has a lot of ten-value cards left in it. But you have to be counting cards to know that.

Still, when you're sitting at the table it sometimes *seems* like a good idea to take insurance. This happens if you've been beaten badly and are feeling especially doomed, or if the dealer hasn't hit a blackjack in a while, or if she's on a run of blackjacks, or if you have a good hand, say a nineteen or twenty, that you'd like a chance to play out, or if you've dumped a huge bet out on a whim and you're suddenly scared the dealer's going to whisk it away by turning over a ten or a face card. In fact, there were dozens of conditions in which we took insurance when we probably shouldn't have. We weren't pros, and we were subject to all the emotional pressures that prey on black-jack players, so we did the stupid thing and tried to protect our bets, telling ourselves that we were just reducing our bets by half, giving away odds.

The casino management had videotapes of our play taken from the cameras mounted in the ceilings, and they said that the dealer had peeked at the hole card and signaled us. The problem was that careful frame-by-frame study of the tapes showed that on almost every occasion we made an insurance bet, we started *before* the dealer peeked, though she often peeked quickly, there's no denying that.

In instances where we did not take insurance, most of the time we made no move to take it, a kind of nonaction that's conventional in casino play if you don't want insurance. A few times we brought money out while we thought about taking insurance, then did not take it.

That's the case in a nutshell. We didn't know the dealer, never had any contact with her, didn't conspire, there were no signals, we lost plenty of money, and she did not profit in any way from this alleged conspiracy. But from a legal point of view, we had to prove a lot of negatives and at the same time explain the whole game to the jury. All the other side had to do was play the tape and holler "See!" from time to time. As far as the prosecutor was concerned, the less the jury knew about the fine points the better.

There's a psychological collapse that tends to occur when you have pushed your bet out — especially when it's a large bet — and the dealer then lays an ace face up in front of her on the table. It flashes through your mind that each deck has sixteen tens, jacks, queens, and kings, almost a third of the available cards. Oh, Jesus, you think. Oh, no. It's as if her blackjack is already a fact. But then you remember insurance, and in spite of having read books that advise against it, it seems like a second chance.

Gambling in general is full of trick psychology and compelling homemade superstitions of all kinds, and going through your mind continually as you bet are seemingly analytical thoughts that are actually parodies of logic. Half the time you're thinking, Well, she had blackjack the last three times, so she can't have it this time. The other half of the time you're thinking, Well, she had it the last three times; she's on a roll; she must have it this time.

We took insurance for every damn-fool reason you could think of. So the pattern of our play was, we suspect, not discernible, and this is likely one of the reasons the casino believed we were cheating. The player who plays for the kind of money we played for would normally be more expert, would play the insurance game better than we did.

17

Law

AFTER BEING INDICTED, arrested, and booked, ignorance of the justice system was no longer a charming naïveté or an artistic flaw of character. We had no idea, in December 1997, just how bad things were, because we had no idea how awkward — how terrifying, clumsy, and remarkably unsupple — the law was. Turns out it's like Dr. Frankenstein's monster: if it manages to get through the door, it does so by accident. But we were cherry and didn't know that. Over the next year, we'd get an education.

About the same time as our booking, Mr. Holleman secured from the district attorney's office the first discovery materials — a thick packet of photocopies. We took copies of these copies home and read though the material cover to cover. This was an ink-and-paper embrace like the embrace of all of the other bureaucracies that had held us since birth; this one was just much nastier.

What was it? A copy of the indictment. Copies of forms from the jailing of the dealer. Copies of pages from the casino's "Standard Procedure Manual," detailing how the dealers were supposed to deal, how to treat the players ("Guests enjoy being known. Try to learn their names . . ."), and so on. Forms titled "86'ED" with our hapless Polaroids from that morning in the little windowless room, all the detail flattened out of them by the photocopy. Eyes: brown. No, got that wrong. Make a note. Goes to the accuracy of their observations.

And on and on. Forms offering us a plea bargain: all we had to do was to plead guilty, quickly, to a felony, make unspecified "restitution," and pay a five-thousand-dollar fine, each of us. For this we would receive probation instead of two years in prison. This was pro forma, we were told; they always offer you the rock-bottom, absolute worst deal to open the bargaining. I see, we said.

Also in the discovery materials was the "evidence." This included various statements from casino employees — the uniformed security guy, the blond shift boss, and others — and a summary written by a Gaming Commission agent. These Statements, Incident Reports, and Case Reports, notwithstanding their official-sounding headings, were a witches' brew of facts, inaccuracies, opinions, fantasies, and freewheeling conjecture.

Accompanying these was a seven- or eight-page handwritten analysis of fifty-odd hands of blackjack, a write-up keyed to two composite — that is, edited — overhead videotapes showing blackjack play on the third and eleventh of November 1996, which the casino and the Gaming Commission alleged showed us cheating.

Much of this handwritten analysis had to do with the dealer's violations of the casino's prescribed routines, noting times when she peeked at her hole card when she apparently wasn't supposed to, mostly when she had an ace up, but also times when she was showing tens, nines, and a three. Aces and tens, she was supposed to look under, according to the manual; the others, not. There was no apparent logic, nefarious or otherwise, in her pattern of looking. Other times, notations said things like, "Signals player to take insurance by fanning cards" or "Nods her head 'no.' "

Sometime later we got copies of the videotapes. What we saw — in black and white — was the tops of our heads, our hands, our shirtsleeves, other players, and the dealer, who was often undeniably quick to look at her hole card in the peeker in front of her. A few times she also slid her cards in a tiny circle before letting them rest on the felt tabletop. It was a little flourish, a bit of dealer style, we guessed, like the patter of a disc jockey or an auctioneer. She had been bored, we guessed. This "fanning" happened about six times in fifty hands.

The other "signals" had been subjected to similarly strenuous interpretation. The notation "Nods her head 'no' " described not a nod but a look: the dealer glanced briefly to the side — she turned her head, near as we could determine by playing the videotape over and over. This notation occurred once, maybe twice.

In the security guy's statement, he writes that the dealer "stressed the word insurance . . . At that point both males knew that they needed insurance to save their bets." Oh, c'mon, we thought. The dealers are supposed to call out "Insurance." The casino manual includes this injunction: "Dealer must say 'Insurance?' in a clearly audible voice."

That was the range of the supposed signals, a little grab bag. If you analyzed them meticulously — as we did when we got the videotapes — they seemed to have shifting, sometimes contradictory meanings. In fact, in some of the hands shown on these composite tapes, the play we make is the *opposite* of what it would've been if the dealer had communicated her hole card. But to see that required painstaking analysis that followed the hands to their conclusion. Someone who had already decided a crime had been committed probably wouldn't bother.

Unfortunately, someone sitting on a jury might not bother, either. It was too complicated a point to argue in a trial, we were given to understand — part of our education in the increasingly terrifying criminal justice system.

That the law wasn't about justice had always been a suspicion, even after years of watching lawyer shows on television, from *Perry Mason* right through *L.A. Law* and *Law and Order*. Watching hogwash, basically. The law wasn't about finding the truth. It wasn't about guilt and innocence. It was about telling the jury a story. And whoever told the best story won. Later, we heard Anthony Hopkins say exactly this in a Spielberg movie.

The whole case would rest on dueling narratives — we had to tell a better story than the other side.

The prosecution's story was that we had been meeting with the dealer, conspiring apparently; that was the inference we drew one afternoon from a call Mr. Holleman made to the assistant district attorney. We listened, sitting in the worn leather chairs in his office. "Hey, Annette," he said, clicking on the speaker phone, "why you always trying to put my good clients in the penitentiary?"

"Only when they're guilty," she said.

The exchange went on for several minutes — good-old-boy, good-old-girl stuff. Then, as we sat looking across his cluttered desk at Mr. Holleman, who was sitting sideways to speak into the machine, we heard her say she could help us if we would tell her how we got hooked up with this dealer.

Suddenly we felt weak. They really believed we knew the dealer, that this was some big conspiracy, some plot. Mr. Holleman was exclaiming into the telephone: "Shoot, they never *met* the dealer. They didn't even *know* this dealer. They've been teaching up at Southern . . . for fifteen, twenty years!"

But it seemed clear that she heard this as more patter, an elaboration of the game they'd been playing, the game they often played.

It became evident that she had read or been told about a statement included in the discovery that said at the time we were thrown out of the Grand, we had cashed in three thousand dollars' worth of chips. What she didn't know, hadn't been told, was that those chips were all that remained of about thirteen thousand dollars' worth that we had bought that night. When the assistant district attorney said something about "all the money they won," Mr. Holleman corrected her impression, told her we hadn't won, we'd lost. But she didn't seem to hear that.

Our trial was scheduled to begin on April 13, 1998, and in March we drove down to Gulfport for a consultation with Mr. Holleman and his son, Tim, a sharp-witted, charming man of about thirty-five, also an attorney, also working on the case. It turned out that the trial was going to be delayed because Mr. Holleman had planned to undergo heart surgery and would still be recovering in April. Summer was a better time for us anyway; we'd have fewer classes, less disturbance at the school.

The trial was rescheduled for late July, and we were relieved. When you go through something like this, you desperately want it to be over, but at the same time you're happy to put it off. Meanwhile, you're thinking about it all the time, night after night, and then it strikes you that the state, the district attorney, hasn't given it a thought for months. None of the people who visited this on you are lying awake at night worrying about it.

Tim Holleman took us to meet a video specialist, and afterward we went to lunch at an Olive Garden. Tim's obvious affection for his father was winning, and his funny stories about the old man in court reminded us of our own father, how his stories had become our memories of him.

Tim told a story about working with his father on a case in which the opposing lawyer repeatedly stooped under the table to look inside a big briefcase while speaking. Mr. Holleman winked at Tim, and when the lawyer went for his briefcase the next time, Mr. Holleman shouted, "I object!" whereupon the surprised lawyer jerked his head up, cracking it against the underside of the table. "Your honor," Mr. Holleman said. "We can't hear counsel when he's down there under that table!" Tim laughed, full of admiration and delight.

Under a barrage of questions from us, Tim mentioned that we *could,* of course, lose — "even innocent people like you lose occasionally. Any time you take it into court," he said, "there's no predicting what a jury might do." Really? We could lose? This was news to us, dull pupils in an ongoing legal education.

We didn't know why the D.A.'s office was pursuing the case. Prosecutors prosecute, Tim said. That's what they do. Sometimes they'd rather try a case and lose than not try it at all.

Later, we asked another lawyer if she agreed, and she did, saying D.A.s are paid to prosecute. Don't they look at the cases? She said they don't have time. They've got cases piled up to their ears. When a court date comes, they take a look at the file and go in and try it and do the best they can. This lawyer told us, "Forget *Law and Order*. Those scenes where everybody sits around and they decide what's best to do, what's the most just thing to do, how best to seek justice? Forget that. That isn't how it happens. There are a bunch of people

in a shabby office and there are files everywhere and eighty
million cases and three-quarters of the cases are dirty and
everybody knows they're dirty."

Our education continued.

We studied the discovery materials and wrote letters to
Tim and Mr. Holleman itemizing flaws, inconsistencies, and
errors in the state's version of the facts. We watched the state-
supplied edited videotapes over and over, in slow motion, taking detailed notes on every blackjack hand — they were all
listed by time, 03:41:33, 03:41:38, etc. — about ninety percent of
which showed our insurance bets already made or in process
when the dealer was peeking at her hole card. We tried to reason the thing out, as our father would have done. We wrote
more letters to the Hollemans, presenting new arguments:
"Why would somebody who was cheating to get a tiny advantage at blackjack then give that advantage away to slot machines?" "If we were conspiring with this woman, why did we
go to the casino and gamble all night on a dozen nights when
she wasn't even there?" Late in the spring, in one of our meet-
ings with the lawyers, we asked if they minded getting all the
letters. "Not if you don't mind us not answering them," Mr.
Holleman said.

When we talked to our lawyers about what we might argue,
what evidence we might show, how we might demonstrate
that the casino's procedures against us weren't kosher, they
said to forget it. We have a simple project, they said. We'll run
the tapes in slow motion, and they will show you're making
bets before she's looked at her cards. Therefore she's got no information about her cards prior to your making your bets, so
there is no information being passed, and there is no conspiracy. It's fact. We just deal with the facts.

That's fine, we said, that sounds like a good idea, but we

want to win this case three or four ways. We'll tell the true story, ambiguous and complex and —

Then Mr. Holleman stopped us. We did *not* want something complicated. We did *not* want a narrative rich in nuance, a narrative with secondary characters and underlying motivations, a narrative with a representation of blackjack play as it takes place in casinos every day. We did not want reality. We wanted a picture you could draw with a child's marker.

This was worrisome. We had watched the O. J. Simpson trial for a year, and that should have wised us up, but it hadn't. You imagine things going wrong, and you imagine ending up in striped pants, picking litter off the highway. It didn't seem likely, but it was possible.

As two people who tended to live and die by our imaginations, the prospect of snagging a Snickers wrapper by the side of the road and putting it into a bag slung over our shoulder while a trusty with a shotgun watched from the seat of the truck was all too real. So we joked about it. We needed jokes. We were scared. Probably more scared than necessary, because it was our business to imagine things thoroughly.

In short, just as being the subject of a reporter's story had given us a new appreciation of journalism, being in the crosshairs of the district attorney had given us a new appreciation of the law: it's something like using a flamethrower to light a cigarette — you'd better watch your face. Perhaps the system is effective against obvious criminals, but the next time we hear somebody saying, "Wait a minute, I didn't do it," we'll think twice before concluding: They caught him, indicted him, tried him, found him guilty; he must have done it.

We had been indicted on a charge of conspiracy that carried with it a possible two-year prison term. Nine months later, in July 1998, the D.A.'s office would file a "superseding indictment" that charged us with two counts of the same conspiracy — one for November 3 and one for November 11, 1996, thereby doubling the potential penalties. Just housecleaning, we were told. And maybe they're trying to scare you a little.

As the new July court date approached, we heard from Tim Holleman that our trial would again be delayed. He offered various reasons. One was that the trial lawyers' annual meeting in Destin, Florida — the beach — was scheduled for late in the month, and nobody wanted to try a case the week before Destin. When is it being rescheduled? Don't know, Tim said. October maybe. It'll probably be October. That was fine by us. Set it after the millennium for all we care.

In September, we drove down to Gulfport to be arraigned on the new two-count indictment. While waiting at the courthouse, we stood outside a courtroom where a voir dire for a murder trial was taking place. Tim went off to hunt up somebody who could expedite our arraignment. We saw a woman we knew, a dealer from one of the casinos, with her family; maybe her kid was in trouble. Some prospective jurors from the murder case wandered into the hall. They held paper paddles with numbers Magic Markered on one side. A skinny guy in a T-shirt and big pants, big sneakers, huddled in urgent conversation with a bigger, fat guy on a bench across from us. The skinny guy was wrought up about something, and his new acquaintance was trying to calm him down, but the skinny guy was not easily placated. "No, man," the fat guy finally said, "I don't think we get paid until *after* we get on the jury."

18

Spotlight

WE HAD TOLD few people about the mess we were in, and by that strategy alone had successfully kept it from becoming general knowledge. We hoped to get it settled in our favor before it became a bonfire. Too often people automatically assume guilt. Indeed, a liberal and enlightened poet at another university, who had once considered Rick for a job, was reported to remark, on learning of the indictment, "Thank God we didn't hire *him!*"

It stayed quiet until early March 1998, when an editor at the *New York Times* assigned the story of our case to a "gambling writer." The editor thought the story was ironic, Rick having published a novel called *Bob the Gambler* and all. The writer flew down to Gulfport, checked right into the Grand Casino's hotel, and was happy to accept the Grand's hospitality *and* its point of view on the case.

When he got Rick on the phone, the reporter presented himself as sympathetic, a true friend, a pal. Rick said that we were innocent, and that was all he could say; talk to our lawyers. The reporter was chatty; it was hard to get off the phone. He said he was coming up to Hattiesburg the next day, could we meet with him? No, we couldn't. Well, he had to come anyway, to talk to the university people. Was Rick sure we didn't want to meet? Is that sort of a threat? Rick asked. What threat? Why no, of course not. What an idea!

The piece appeared on March 7, 1998, on the front page of the *Times*. Irony was noted in a picture caption. According to the story, the prosecutors wouldn't talk to the reporter. He never talked to Steve, and Rick had said almost nothing of substance to him. He did talk to our employer, people we work with, our students, and, most cordially, to the casino management. He's one of the paper's gambling writers, after all.

The article said: "According to court documents and people involved in the case, the two men were in the casino more than a year ago when surveillance cameras observed them receiving signals from the dealer and being paid for hands they did not win — a practice known as 'dumping the game.'"

Wrong. We were *accused* of getting signals, but not the rest. "Dumping the game" must have come from "people involved in the case" — that is, not from us, not from the D.A., who had declined to talk, but from casino or Gaming Commission people, the same ones who created the "court documents" in the first place.

And isn't "observed them receiving signals" a conclusion, an interpretation of what the cameras recorded? Did the reporter simply accept the casino's interpretation and print it as fact?

Next, *People* magazine called, and so did *48 Hours* and CNN and others, and over the next month every newspaper from Kalamazoo to Calcutta printed a version of the *Times* story. "According to the *New York Times*," many of them said, replacing the authority of "people involved in the case" with that of the *Times*.

Happily, Mississippi's coastal papers and the Jackson paper did rewrites restoring some of the doubt about our guilt that the *Times* had seen fit to leave out, and our local TV stations carried the news as well, calling us "Fredericka and Steven Barthelme."

In late spring, *People* sent someone to do an interview. The person it sent was the whistleblower Ron Ridenhour, the man who first revealed the My Lai tragedy during the Vietnam War. He was living in New Orleans and worked as a stringer for *People* while researching several stories he hoped to write about at length. Meeting him before his sudden death, in May of 1998, was one of the few events that made this period bearable. He was kind, funny, serious, and generous, all at the same time.

Fifteen months after the indictment, in the spring of 1999, we were still awaiting trial on the felony charges. Our new life adrift in the legal system and our nightlife in the casinos soon seemed eerily parallel. Both were places we had never been. Both were fierce, slow, illogical, incoherent. Both provided erratically rising and falling anxiety as we were jerked this way and that, by law and by cards, producing euphoria and dread in capricious sequence, feelings that were out of our ken and not all that distinct, one from the other. We felt almost as if we were sleeping, that neither the casinos nor the lawyers were real, that the consequences, however terrifying, were hallucinations. Full of queer physics, odd rules, these were dreams of falling. We struggled to think straight, failed.

Indictments were all the rage on television news. We'd never had much reason to pay attention before, but now every time someone said "indictment," we listened up. Like many middle-class folk, we had, in our inattention, come to equate "indicted" with "guilty." When our mess became public, some people we knew seemed to reflect the same equation. Old friends stumbled around with the problem, getting it right eventually.

We noticed things people said in casual conversation, at parties or over dinner, in interviews on television, things mentioned in news magazines and in movies and on TV shows with lawyers in them. We listened with growing dread. In 1998 we stopped watching a favorite TV show, *Michael Hayes*, because its lead character, a federal prosecutor, always won. The accused were always guilty. Hayes always got them before the credits ran. On his show you not only waited for the presumption of innocence to come to an end, you could barely find it. This no longer seemed fun to us. *His* indictments always turned into convictions.

By contrast, *The Practice* became a new favorite. We loved this show, loved it with hope, with our futures in mind. Bobby Donnell, Eugene, Lindsey, Jimmy, Ellenor, Rebecca, and Helen, dear Helen — these characters couldn't have been more cherished. *The Practice* was full of decent people who cared about others, who wanted to do a little good if they could, who didn't want to do any harm. On both sides of the courtroom, defense and prosecution, the practitioners were thoughtful, passionate, and compassionate. Some of the criminals weren't even criminals. The idea of innocence floated around the show like a blessing. It was a wonderful world, the kind of world we wanted to be part of.

We wanted our lawyers to be just like this cast of characters — earnest, careful, clever, quick, thoughtful. Winners. The indicted, the accused, always went free, because they were most often innocent, and because of the handsome lawyering of the gang. We watched it religiously.

*

In the months after November 1997, when we first thought about our indictment, about being criminals, felons, it was interesting. In a tiny way, we were suddenly "made" guys. "Felon" was a word we'd heard on TV since we were kids, a word from some other world, a place where evil dwelt, where shadowy figures met in rundown rooms under bare bulbs, light chains swinging, lots of undershirts in evidence. It was so far off our beaten path that we felt we'd been dropped into another galaxy. And it was romantic in its way — the dark, brooding felons brooding darkly at the grocery store. That sort of thing. We imagined people giving us a slightly wider berth because of our newfound criminal dimension. We were *serious* in ways the unaccused can never hope to be.

But being charged had already cost us considerable pain and was certain to cost more. It might mean our jobs. Our ordinary lives suddenly had too much sizzle — how were we to get back to that precious land where they didn't? Like a lot of people, we had taken things for granted, taken almost everything for granted. Now the business we'd taken for granted was threatened by an arrest and charges that, no matter how ridiculous, weren't going to vanish. Law doesn't work that way; it doesn't say "oops" very often.

So we were stuck with somebody's idea of a joke. Daily life, the whole sad self of it, now meant something to us, meant not being under indictment, not being threatened with trial or prison or public humiliation. Our perspectives changed. We cared more about things we used to make fun of; we had a greater distaste for the easy puffing of folks trying day after day to make themselves important, and at the same time we found them a bit more in our hearts.

Sometimes we wondered what it would be like a year later, a year after it was over. We were certain there would be an after, and there was some solace in that. We hadn't resolved to live our lives differently, but we'd thought about it. We'd resolved to do things better. One of our graduate students, upon receiving an important award, said she had begun wearing her seat belt for the first time.

That was exactly why she got the award, because she could see the relationship between wearing her seat belt and getting the award — the prospect of a future, the willingness to do things right, the hope implicit in restraint.

19

Father

OUR FATHER LIVED FOR sixteen months after Mother died. His life during that time, especially the last seven months, was bad, and where we might have eased that, we did not do enough. We failed him. Our love for our father, unlike that for Mother, was largely abstract. We didn't love him less, but the love existed in our heads first, our hearts after. We loved the *idea* of Father. It was the idea that was dear and necessary. It was the idea of Father that, since childhood, had occupied the place opposite Mother's personal, physical presence.

Loving him personally was harder. Our relationship with him had not only been abstract, it also often felt like that of student and teacher or employee and boss, and Father could be harsh with those he taught or hired. Helping him was not simple. Our help was always in danger of not measuring up, of requiring an ungentle adjustment or correction, which had the feeling, the smell, the threat of rejection. We were, in an instant, and for a cause so tiny as to be inexplicable, dull-witted. Maybe he didn't know this was the effect of his manner, but he should have known. Eighteen years of this as children, and another thirty as adults, made us wary of just rolling up our sleeves. He had always been demanding, often blunt, sometimes irascible. Age and infirmity had not cured him; at eighty-nine, his people skills had not improved.

He was an overweight, hypochondriac, weakening old man, but we were still leery of him, so any little argument — about staying on his telephone too long, say, or how much a visiting nurse ought to charge, or what was a living wage nowadays — had our sense of self at risk in it. At the same time, we didn't want to admit his decay; our idea of him could not abide it. We had the choice of bullying this weak, failing, but obstinate old man, forcing him — and ourselves — into an ever greater awareness of his diminished powers, or acquiescing as we had always done.

Father's relations with others had always been distant, by his own design and insistence. He seemed not to need them much. He liked an audience, but showed little want of companions. About five years before he died, Father, out for a walk, slipped on some ice on a speed bump in the apartment complex's parking lot and broke his ankle. This occurred late in December, so we were in Houston at the time. He went into the hospital for surgery on the ankle, which involved installing metal screws in his bones. We and our mother paced the corridors, waiting for him to emerge from the anesthesia, wondering what was taking so long. Then he was out, in a hospital room. He wanted a few things from the house, he said, but no visitors, not even Mother. Visiting the sick struck him as a waste of time, an uncomfortable, often false social exercise.

"You're just saying that," Mother said. But he wasn't. He preferred to lie in his hospital bed alone all day.

At a stretch, we admired him for it, this blunt honesty. He

had things he believed in and things he lived by, and he paid for them; frequently he lost work or gave up career advancement for telling people what he thought. Often the stories Father told us concerned those occasions, how those things had happened. Although by his old age he had worn them out, having told them too many times, we had a residual affection for these heroic tales of his career. How he always did the "right thing"; how, when he said fourteen inches on center, he *meant* fourteen inches on center; how he wouldn't have specified glass seventeen thirty-seconds of an inch thick if he didn't need every thirty-second of an inch; and how the contractor who installed the half-inch glass instead was either foolish or worse, and in the end lost three hundred thousand dollars for his mistake. In some sense, these stories are what he left us. That story about Mies van der Rohe's explanation of his contentment at being able to make things beautiful, and Father's image of himself as surprised, nonplused — "He had given me a lesson." Another story about Louis Kahn, after hours, going around the architectural office in which they had both worked in Philadelphia, leaving critiques on all their coworkers' designs. "They laughed at him," Father said, "when they found the little pieces of drafting paper the next morning. But Louis was teaching himself." In yet another story, Father, at fifty or fifty-five, jumped up and down on a concrete bench outside a school he had designed. The concrete broke in half. This was done to demonstrate to a contractor that he had positioned the reinforcing steel in the wrong place, too low in the concrete slab where it added too little strength, and that the bench might break. The contractor's second mistake had been arguing with Father. How Father knew the steel was below the middle of the slab, we don't remember. He guessed, we guess.

There were lots of stories like these, told again and again, illustrating our beloved idea of our beloved father.

Nine months after Mother died, around Christmas 1995, we went to Houston to see Father, and in the ten days we were there he went from reasonable health to being an invalid. He was suddenly infirm and insisted on being taken care of.

It wasn't that he couldn't function. It wasn't that he couldn't take care of himself. It seemed as if he didn't *want* to take care of himself. He complained at great length about taking a bath or a shower. He was afraid he might fall. He complained about shaving, how difficult it was with an electric razor. He was giving up, which seemed inconceivable to us.

He complained about never getting anything organized and about falling behind in his reading. His office was filled with the magazines he subscribed to — *Discovery, Scientific American, Nature,* architectural magazines, *Time, Newsweek, The New Yorker,* photography magazines. There were stacks on his desk twenty magazines high, issues he hadn't gotten to yet. He wouldn't throw them away, and he wouldn't read them. Whenever he got a new one in the mail he'd put it on the stack. Going to get the mail was a chore, a half-mile walk out and back through the big apartment complex. His legs were tired, and he didn't want to walk. When we'd arrived for Christmas, he was walking, though grabbing doorframes and making theatrical *oh*s here and there as he progressed. There was something dubious about this new incapacity; it seemed to come and go. Still, when we left a week and a half later, he had decided that he could not walk at all, and he was in a wheelchair.

It was a peculiar psychological gesture, we thought, as if he were not walking to demonstrate just how old and frail he was, how much he needed our help. What he didn't reckon on was that we had been trained by him, and that his answer to that kind of demonstrated incapacity had always been, "Relax. Get a grip on yourself." Which is essentially what we said, in the form of a wheelchair, providing the apparatus for rolling around the house while at the same time discouraging it.

We thought the wheelchair was bad, fearing that if he stopped walking for a while, he'd stop forever, losing whatever strength his legs had. Twenty-five years before, we had listened with dread from another room as Father had forced *his* mother up from a bed to walk around in the house, for the exercise. She was then ninety-two, failing fast, and screeching and crying, fighting to be left alone. He may have been right then, but that sound in memory didn't make us want to force him up, even if we could have.

Our attempts to help him in the last part of his life did not go well. We thought a great deal about Father and what was to be done, had several ideas in fact, including moving him to Hattiesburg, an idea that Father had no interest in at Christmastime, but would later think about again.

What we did at Christmas was ride around with Joan, looking at a number of places he might stay — those wretched nursing homes where we all promise never to put our parents. Some were better than others; most were the same ones we'd looked at a year earlier for Mother, when we didn't know she was going to die.

Pete planned to move from Houston to Seadrift, one hundred and fifty miles down the Texas coast, in January of 1996. Joan was leaving Pennzoil and moving to Virginia in May. After that, no one would be left in Houston to take care of Father.

After we returned to Hattiesburg in January, Pete and Joan made extraordinary efforts to find Father a suitable living situation — either a place he could abide and where there were people to help him or some arrangement for him to stay in his apartment, with people coming in to cook and clean and care for him. Joan lined up hospital-sponsored organizations, then private enterprises to do the work. She set these arrangements in motion while she was still in town so that she could keep an eye on them.

Of course nothing was satisfactory to Father. It was a no-win situation. She could not possibly please him with these arrangements, no matter how wonderful they might have been. First there was the matter of money — who was going to pay? He was by this time nuts about money. He thought fifty dollars a day for full-time home care was ridiculously high, so that was out. And if Father was going to pay for a nursing home, how much was it going to cost? And oh, that was too much as well. If Joan were going to pay, well, that was an admission that she had more money than he. No good acknowledging that.

We participated in this planning when we were in Houston, but more over the long-distance telephone in consultations with Joan and Pete. And we had complicated conversations with Father.

On occasion, it seemed Joan had persuaded Father to try a nursing home, one she and Rick had visited the year before. It was a fatiguing place, a kind of hospital stripped of medical authority and the magic of healing — the official doctor making rounds, nurses striding about taking care of things, the sense of important healthful business being transacted. The nursing home had none of that. These were little white rooms laid out like a stockyard, full of people bent at the waist, weeping in their beds, calling out to absent friends or relatives.

Of the homes we visited, some of them quite pricey, this was the least grotesque. But there was nothing particularly inviting or comfortable or kind about it. It would do the job. Minimally trained people worked the floors in three shifts; they could help Father with whatever problem he might have — be it washing or moving or getting a meal.

Joan brought Father to look at the place two different times during the spring of 1996. On the first visit, he left without a word moments after he arrived. But he went back another day, saying he hadn't given the place a fair chance. He rolled solemnly through the halls in his wheelchair, looking into each of the rooms, one after another, we were told. When he finished the complete circuit, he indicated he was ready to go back to the car. Joan drove him home.

That night he told Joan he wanted to arrange for someone to come to his townhouse. The nursing home was too depressing, and for whatever period he needed someone, he could pay the price and put up with another person in the house.

This pleased us all because it seemed the most comfortable resolution. He was figuring a person could come in four or five hours a day, three days a week, and that would be sufficient. She — it would be a she — could leave a meal for him when she left, allowing him to sleep until noon the next day. She could help him wash and change, and help with medications as needed.

Before Joan left for Virginia in May, she hired a private home-care service on these terms, readying second and third sources should the first go sour. Father seemed reasonably happy with this arrangement. He appeared to like the first woman who came in, though of course she got in his hair, as he said, all the time. She constantly asked him questions: did he want this or that, what did he want for dinner? He couldn't abide these in-

terruptions. He snapped at her. As often happens with in-home care, a new person had to be sent periodically to replace the one he could no longer stand having in the house.

Eventually the first service bailed out and was replaced with the second on Joan's list. Some of the workers seemed to have odd ways of behaving. Once, when a man was sent, he apparently went upstairs and stayed there all day long while Father was downstairs. Late in the afternoon, he came down with the family Bible and wanted to read to Father from it.

But from Hattiesburg it seemed that his problems, while not solved, were at least temporarily at bay. In our conversations with him, which were frequent, sometimes four or five times a week, he seemed to be making do. Later that spring, he had a bed moved downstairs and rearranged the first floor of the apartment so that he never had to go upstairs. Files and bills and financial materials were moved down too. The living room furniture was stacked in the dining room so that the living room could be his bed-sitting room. He still had a few Aalto chairs and the low Saarinen chair he had always liked, but now he also had bedpans and Depends, two walkers, a wheelchair, and a dining table full of business papers.

But there was no business. He had nothing to do. Soon enough he recognized that, then found himself incapable of doing anything. His ability to focus on any project, to understand what that project might be, seemed to elude him, and by the summer of 1996 most of his routines for functioning, for survival, had vanished. Worse, he knew it.

He told us he would pick up a folder on the table, roll around the table in his wheelchair, and place it somewhere else. Pick up the folder from there and replace it where he had started from. Open the folder and leaf through it, then call one of us on the phone. He would chat with us about some problem with insurance or mutual funds or government bonds. Moments after he began a conversation, he'd be on to another subject. He wondered where he was going to live or whom he should live with. Didn't we want him to come live with us?

The truth was we didn't. We talked about it, trying to persuade ourselves to do it anyway, as it more and more seemed necessary. Guilty, we rationalized, equivocated, argued — ungrateful children hiding their unwillingness to take care of an aging parent. He was doing all right, we told each other. It might be worse for him here, we said. To explain our reluctance, we used the fiction about the little boy who cried wolf. Father, at eighty-nine, was the little boy. We were the wolves.

We thought we loved our father very much when in fact we were only two people who forgave him all his peculiarities, all his arrogance and authoritarian rule, his cruel and stupid behavior, which we never thought was meant to hurt. There were other views in the family, ideas that this cruelty was intentional, or a kind of power positioning — Father desperately trying to maintain control over his world, over his children if no one else.

Rather, it was our sense that Father was ingenious but socially inept. That he was goodhearted even in his most cruel-seeming behavior toward our mother, the cruelty a byproduct of his way of knowing the world, which was, simply put, that the world was a place that needed fixing and he was just the man to fix it.

Mother drove him crazy near the end of her life. He was desperate to help her, but his ideas for that help were monstrous and unthinkable. She wanted to take an aspirin at night to help her sleep, and somehow he got it into his head that this in part was causing her mental problems, problems that had been carefully diagnosed and were being treated, insofar as treatment was possible. But Father went on an aspirin crusade, hid the bottles from her, counting out how many she took, often refused to give her one when she felt she needed it. He thought he had good reason; there was madness in him then.

They got a housekeeper, and Mother liked to go downstairs and talk to her about the dinner preparations, but to Father this was deeply wrong — you did not interfere with someone who was working. He would not allow her to go downstairs. And all the time he was telling us that Mother was driving him nuts.

But while we often got angry with him, even confronted him with this anger, the effects of it were never long-lived, with us or him.

He was a complicated man, an unusual man, exceedingly bright and driven, controlling and controlled by his own vision of the way things might be. This vision was always, in our view, benevolent, though it often appeared anything but. In the end, it was we who failed our father, not our father who failed us. We were not there when he died. We did not provide enough love and affection, support and care. We provided nothing sufficient to his needs.

We had the ready example of our mother the year before, for whom we had provided all of those things, and thus there was no reasonable way to sidestep the truth about our father's bad death.

This is not to say that Father was unattended during his last days. Pete was at the house the night before Father died. Rick talked to him the night before he died. Joan talked to him two days before, as did Steve. It's just that our attention wasn't sufficient. It wasn't heartfelt, thorough, caring enough. We did not offer ourselves, probably at least in part because we feared he'd eat us alive. He could do that. Makes us wilt with fear.

In the middle of the night on July 16, 1996, Father got tangled up trying to get out of the wheelchair and into his bed. His leg caught in the wheelchair somehow, and he toppled forward onto the bed with his head and torso on the mattress, face down, and the rest of his body twisted, perhaps painfully, in the mechanical apparatus of the chair's arm and wheel. He stayed all night in that condition. He was found in the morning by the woman who was taking care of him, who knocked on the door as usual and, when no one answered, went to get a security guard to let her in.

Father was alive when she found him. She got him into bed, on his back, and left him resting. When she returned an hour later, he was dead.

His death in these slightly peculiar circumstances haunts us both. The thought that a simple thing — moving him to Hattiesburg — might have avoided this altogether. He might be alive today. He was not greatly ill otherwise. He had a heart condition, but it was manageable. If he'd had a couple of decent sons to take care of him, to do his bidding, well, he might have lived. Maybe that was what we were supposed to do. Maybe that's what a good child does. We would have done that — we tried to do it — for Mother, but we would not do it for him.

20

At Last

A FTER FATHER'S DEATH in July, and the trip to Houston
to empty his apartment and dispatch his things and take
over the disposition of his estate, our gambling started up
again in earnest. Trips multiplied. Losses multiplied. Twelve-
hundred-dollar losses became twenty-five-hundred-dollar,
five-thousand-dollar losses. He left each of us about one hundred and fifty thousand dollars, and in the three months between his death and the day we were muscled out of the
casino, we used that money to pay off gambling debts, and we
lost, together, much more. It was as if the money were burning
our hands, burning our imaginations, burning our lives, as if
the loss and guilt were too much to bear and the money was
therefore also too much to bear. We went to the casino at all
hours of the day and night. We stayed days at a time.

Between the beginning of August and November 11, 1996,
we visited the casino sometimes three times a week, two- and
three-day trips. In that period, we lost just over eighty thousand dollars. We loved the place. We liked the friendly smiles
on the dealers' faces, the friendly greetings from the pit bosses,
the sideways inside jokes people made that seemed to say,

You're one of us, you guys belong here. We loved all that. We knew better, but sometimes the satisfaction of being taken for a ride exceeds the satisfaction of knowing you haven't been. That is, it's more fun to go for the ride, no matter how you get there or what the cost.

The psychiatrist who works at the bus stop would have a field day with us — guilt, depression, loss, loneliness, destroying the inheritance. But that doesn't take into account the seductiveness of gambling itself. The excitement. The giddy, foolish mindlessness. To go there and lose felt strangely heroic. How crazy we were being, how bad, how stupid. It's easy to diminish this magic in hindsight, but at the time we were deeply in its thrall. It was a remarkably powerful and seductive bit of theater, with real and bitter consequences, consequences that we wanted. We would have been willing to win, but we were content to lose.

We were the last two of their children, and the idea of our parents' deaths had occurred to us long before. Steve can recall being nine, looking out the playroom window through the empty carport, waiting for his mother to get home, hearing sirens in the distance, fearful. By the time we were twenty-five or so, our parents were deep into their sixties. By the 1990s we'd been worrying that something might happen, anticipating a terrible telephone message for twenty years or more. There was a sense in which we were worn out with it.

In some measure any family ends when the children reach adulthood and start new families of their own. We hadn't done that. We had girlfriends and wives and dogs and cats, but no new families, so the illusion of an enduring one in which we had grown up was precious. We had nothing to replace it with. We had no reason to accumulate wealth, move to a

fancier school district, buy a house, plan a future. If we inherited money, there was nothing to do with it but buy more
things.

We loved Mother better, but after she died, Father still lived,
so the family lived too, or so it seemed. When Father died,
what his death ended was the *illusion* of the family, the fact of
which had vanished years before. With no children, we had
tried to use that illusion as a last shield between ourselves and
the sad vacancy of living.

Worse than the worst left-wing zealot or rose-lensed Polly-
anna, worse than Candide, we didn't want to believe life was
solitary, poor, nasty, brutish, and short, and as children, thanks
to two people, we hadn't had to.

That perfect love which if one is very lucky as a child one has
for one's parents may get smarter, wiser, greater. It may even
get fuller. It never gets any purer. It doesn't move toward perfection, but away. Like everything else, as soon as you find it,
you start losing it.

When you're nine, looking out the window of your parents'
house, listening with dread to ambulance or police sirens, you
might be afraid that your mother or your father has been hurt,
but you're worrying about the wrong thing. They're disap-
pearing from you in a much slower way. By the time you're
twenty-five or thirty, your relationship with them may be loving, but it's certain to be incoherent, and it's likely to be false.
It's certain to be less than it was. At forty, fifty, less again. In our
lives, with no children, no future, just a permanent present, we
believed in the illusion that we could ignore this loss, that the
family was abiding, still mattered. But we were wrong. Our
parents' deaths — Father's more than Mother's, but Mother's
too — were the deaths of mysterious strangers. We did not

know that until it was all over, after the deaths and the gambling and the troubles with the law, and even then we weren't quite certain. But we were sure it was not a thing we wanted to think about. We would think of it later. In the meantime, at the casino, as long as there was money to play with, we never had to think about anything but the cards, and in the cards, everything else disappeared.